5A

Reach
HIGHER

Practice Book

Australia · Brazil · Mexico · Singapore · United Kingdom · United States

NATIONAL GEOGRAPHIC
L E A R N I N G

National Geographic Learning,
a Cengage Company

Reach Higher Practice Book 5A

Publisher, Content-based English: Erik Gundersen

Associate Director, R&D: Barnaby Pelter

Senior Development Editors:
  Jacqueline Eu
  Ranjini Fonseka
  Kelsey Zhang

Development Editor: Rayne Ngoi

Director of Global Marketing: Ian Martin

Heads of Regional Marketing:
  Charlotte Ellis (Europe, Middle East and Africa)
  Kiel Hamm (Asia)
  Irina Pereyra (Latin America)

Product Marketing Manager: David Spain

Senior Production Controller: Tan Jin Hock

Senior Media Researcher (Covers): Leila Hishmeh

Senior Designer: Lisa Trager

Director, Operations: Jason Seigel

Operations Support:
  Rebecca Barbush
  Drew Robertson
  Caroline Stephenson
  Nicholas Yeaton

Manufacturing Planner: Mary Beth Hennebury

Publishing Consultancy and Composition:
  MPS North America LLC

For permission to use material from this text or product,
submit all requests online at **cengage.com/permissions**
Further permissions questions can be emailed to
permissionrequest@cengage.com

ISBN-13: 978-0-357-36700-1

National Geographic Learning
200 Pier Four Blvd
Boston, MA 02210
USA

Locate your local office at **international.cengage.com/region**

Visit National Geographic Learning online at **ELTNGL.com**
Visit our corporate website at **www.cengage.com**

Printed in the United States of America
Print Number: 02   Print Year: 2021

Contents

Unit 1: Crossing Between Cultures

Part 1

Unit 1 Concept Map 1.1

Thinking Map:
  Character Development Chart 1.2

Grammar: Complete Subject and Predicate . . 1.3

Key Points Reading:
  "My Diary Across Places and Time" 1.4

Grammar: Simple Subject and Predicate 1.5

Vocabulary: Apply Word Knowledge 1.6

Reread and Retell:
  Character Development Chart 1.7

Fluency: Expression 1.8

Reading Options: Reflection Journal 1.9

Respond and Extend: Venn Diagram 1.10

Grammar: Complete Sentences 1.11

Part 2

Thinking Map: Venn Diagram 1.12

Grammar: Compound Subjects 1.13

Key Points Reading:
  "A Writer's Journey" 1.14

Grammar: Compound Predicates 1.15

Vocabulary: Apply Word Knowledge 1.16

Reread and Retell: Venn Diagram 1.17

Fluency: Expression 1.18

Reading Options: Dialogue Journal 1.19

Respond and Extend: Comparison Chart 1.20

Grammar: Compound Subjects 1.21

Writing Project:
  Write a Personal Narrative 1.22

Unit 2: Catching the Light

Part 1

Unit 2 Concept Map 2.1

Thinking Map: Character Chart 2.2

Grammar: Kinds of Sentences 2.3

Key Points Reading: "Ten Suns" 2.4

Grammar:
  Questions: *Do/Does; Yes/No* Answers 2.5

Reread and Retell: Character Chart 2.6

Fluency: Intonation 2.7

Reading Options: Reflection Journal 2.8

Respond and Extend: Comparison Chart . . . 2.9

Grammar: Kinds of Sentences 2.10

Part 2

Thinking Map: Goal-and-Outcome Chart . . . 2.11

Grammar: Compound Sentences 2.12

Key Points Reading: "Energy for the Future" . . 2.13

Grammar:
  Compound and Complex Sentences 2.14

Reread and Retell:
  Goal-and-Outcome Chart 2.15

Fluency: Phrasing 2.16

Reading Options: Reflection Journal 2.17

Respond and Extend: Comparison Chart 2.18

Grammar:
  Compound and Complex Sentences 2.19

Writing Project: Write a Myth 2.20

Unit 3: Nature's Webs

Part 1

Unit 3 Concept Map 3.1

Thinking Map: Plot Diagram 3.2

Grammar: Nouns 3.3

Key Points Reading:

  "Coyote and Badger" 3.4

Grammar: Plural Nouns. 3.5

Vocabulary: Apply Word Knowledge 3.6

Reread and Retell: Plot Diagram 3.7

Fluency: Intonation 3.8

Reading Options: K-W-L-Q Chart 3.9

Respond and Extend: Food Web 3.10

Grammar: Plural Nouns 3.11

Part 2

Thinking Map: Tree Diagram 3.12

Grammar: Count/Noncount Nouns 3.13

Key Points Reading: "Fish of the Future" 3.14

Grammar: Irregular Plurals. 3.15

Reread and Retell: Tree Diagram 3.16

Fluency: Expression 3.17

Reading Options: Fact Cards 3.18

Respond and Extend: Comparison Chart . . . 3.19

Grammar: More Plural Nouns 3.20

Writing Project: Write an Interview 3.21

Unit 4: Justice

Part 1

Unit 4 Concept Map 4.1

Thinking Map: Theme Chart 4.2

Grammar: Present Tense Action Verbs 4.3

Key Points Reading: "Crossing Bok Chitto" . . . 4.4

Grammar: Action Verbs:

  Present Progressive 4.5

Reread and Retell: Theme Chart 4.6

Fluency: Expression 4.7

Reading Options: Fact Cards 4.8

Respond and Extend: Comparison Chart . . . 4.9

Grammar: Present Tense Action Verbs 4.10

Part 2

Thinking Map: Sequence Chain 4.11

Grammar: Verbs *am, is, are* 4.12

Key Points Reading: "The Troublemaker" 4.13

Grammar: Verbs *have* and *has*. 4.14

Reread and Retell: Sequence Chain 4.15

Fluency: Phrasing 4.16

Reading Options: Reflection Journal 4.17

Respond and Extend: Comparison Chart . . . 4.18

Grammar: Forms of *be* and *have* 4.19

Writing Project: Write a Research Report 4.20

Photographic Credits 4.26

Name _____ Date _____

Crossing Between Cultures

Make a concept map with the answers to the Big Question:
How can where you are change who you are?

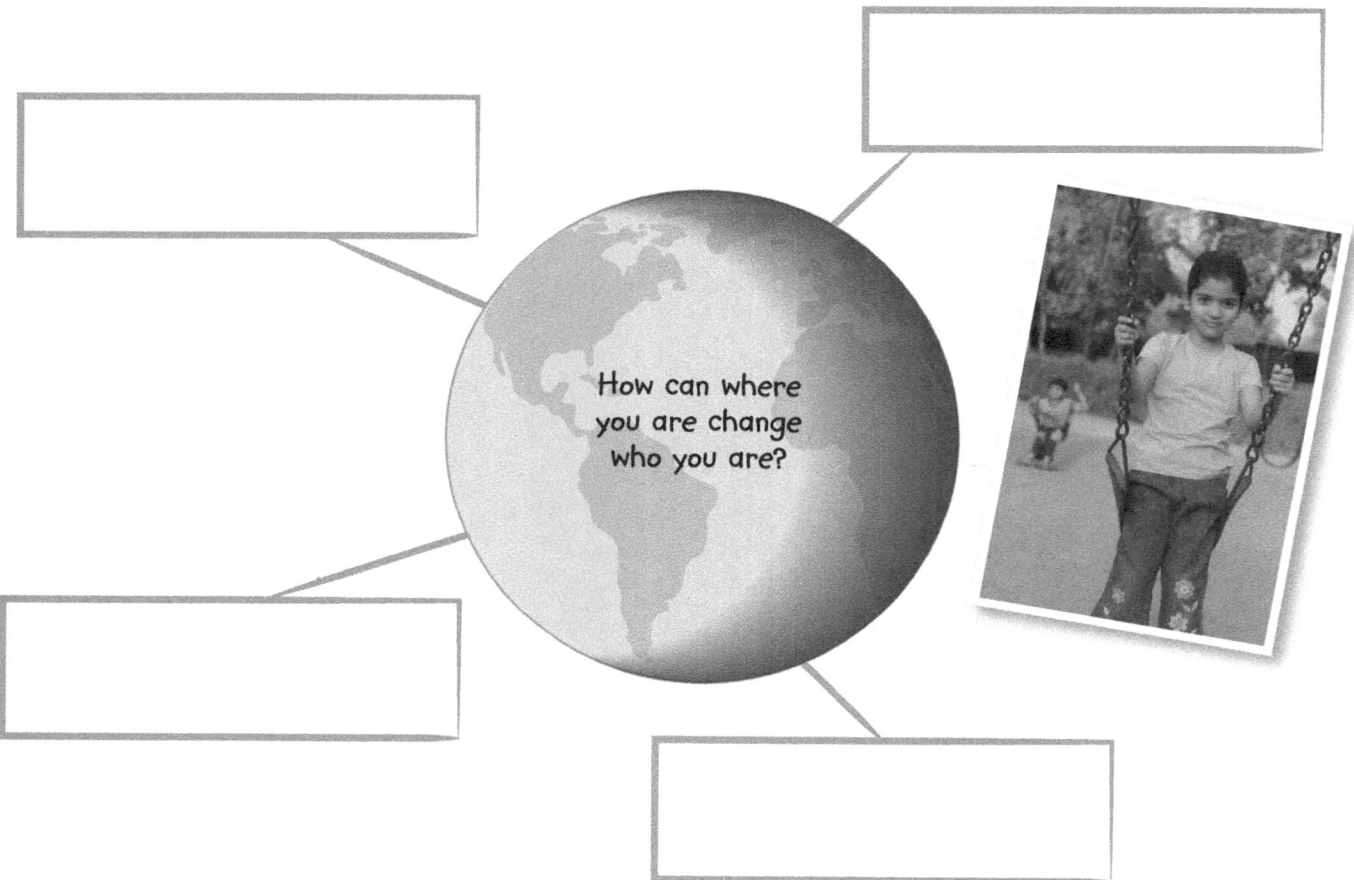

How can where you are change who you are?

Name _____   Date _____

How a Character Changes

Complete a chart about a story in which the character changed.

Beginning	Middle	End

Use this chart to tell about a partner's favorite story. How does the character feel at first? How do the character's feelings change?

Grammar

A New Sport

Grammar Rules Complete Subject and Predicate

1. The **complete subject** includes all the words that describe the subject.

2. The **complete predicate** includes the verb and all the words in the predicate.

Underline the complete subject. Circle the complete predicate.

1. My family and I moved to the United States.

2. We stayed with my aunt and uncle.

3. A boy named Mike lived next door.

4. Mike and his friends taught me how to play basketball.

5. Now basketball is one of my favorite sports.

 **Write a sentence about a culture you know and read it to a partner. Have a partner name the complete subject and complete predicate.**

Name _____   Date _____

"My Diary Across Places and Time"

Listen as your teacher reads. Follow with your finger.

1 Aberto learns his family is moving from New Jersey in the United States back to Brazil. He has lived in the United States for five years and is sad to leave. He worries that he won't remember how to speak Portuguese and wonders where he will go to school.

2 Aberto and his family drive to Brazil in their van and bus. While they are driving, Aberto's dad explains that he needs his help with his new business plan in Brazil. Aberto is excited to help his dad but feels nervous about talking in a language he is not familiar with.

3 Aberto and his family arrive at his grandparents' house in Rio de Janeiro. Aberto still thinks about what he left behind in New Jersey, but realizes that his old life and friend, Hugo, will be in his memory, captured in the pages he writes in his diary.

Grammar

Find Those Parts!

Grammar Rules Simple Subject and Predicate

1. The **simple subject** is the most important noun in the <u>**complete subject**</u>.
2. The **simple predicate** is the verb.

Work with a team of four to complete this task.

1. The first person underlines the simple subject.

My older brother likes spaghetti with tomato sauce.

2. The second person circles the complete subject.

My older brother likes spaghetti with tomato sauce.

3. The third person draws a star over the simple predicate.

My older brother likes spaghetti with tomato sauce.

4. The fourth person draws two lines under the complete predicate.

My older brother likes spaghetti with tomato sauce.

Now try it with these sentences.

- Our grandmother cooks the best rice and tofu dishes.
- My friends want hot dogs.
- Our uncle misses the bread from his town in Italy.

Vocabulary

Vocabulary Bingo

Play Bingo using the Key Words from this unit.

Name _____   Date _____

"My Diary Across Places and Time"

Complete the character development chart for "My Diary Across Places and Time."

Beginning	Middle	End
Aberto is scared and worried about having to move.		

Use the chart to talk about Aberto's story and to retell the story to a partner.

© Cengage Learning, Inc.

Fluency

"My Diary Across Places and Time"

Use this passage to practice reading with proper expression.

Mom broke the news at breakfast after Dad left for work.	11
"You know how much your father loves his job," she said.	22
"He was a great soccer player, and then he worked hard to	34
become a coach, organizing soccer camps for children in this	44
country. Now he wants to move his soccer camps to Brazil,	55
our homeland." Then, Mom added, "Your grandparents are	63
growing old, as well. Try to understand."	70
Why didn't my sisters feel sad, like I did?	79

From "My Diary Across Places and Time," page 14

Expression

B ☐ Does not read with feeling.

I ☐ Reads with some feeling, but does not match content.

A ☐ Reads with appropriate feeling for most content.

AH ☐ Reads with appropriate feeling for all content.

Accuracy and Rate Formula

Use the formula to measure a reader's accuracy and rate while reading aloud.

$$\underline{\hspace{2cm}} - \underline{\hspace{2cm}} = \underline{\hspace{2cm}}$$

words attempted in one minute	number of errors	words correct per minute (wcpm)

Name _____   Date _____

"I Was Dreaming to Come to America"

Complete this reflection journal as you read the oral history.

Page	My question	The answer

 **Ask a partner one of your questions. Then try to answer a partner's question.**

Respond and Extend

Compare Genres

Use a Venn diagram to compare fiction and nonfiction.

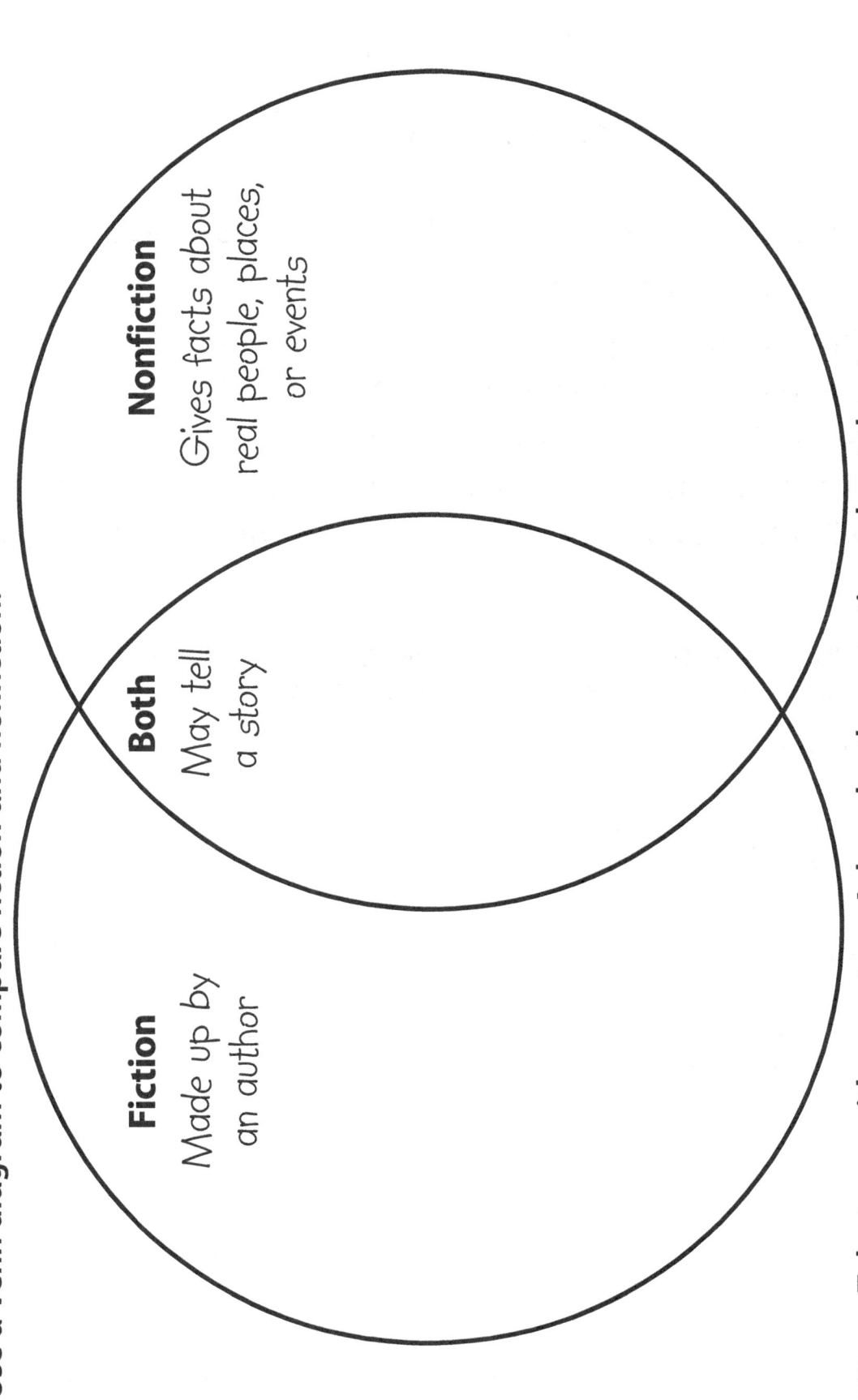

Nonfiction
Gives facts about real people, places, or events

Both
May tell a story

Fiction
Made up by an author

Take turns with a partner. Ask each other questions about the story and the oral history. Complete the Venn diagram.

Name _____   Date _____

Grammar Rules Complete Sentences

1. A sentence must have a **subject** and a **predicate**.
  His favorite grandmother _makes good Korean food._

2. The **simple subject** is what or whom the sentence is about:
  grandmother. The **complete subject** tells more about that
  subject: _His favorite grandmother._

3. The **simple predicate** is the verb: _makes._ The **complete predicate**
  tells more about the predicate: _makes good Korean food._

**Read each group of words. Add a subject or a predicate to write a
complete sentence. Use correct punctuation.**

1. came to visit

  She came to visit. _____

2. Greg's whole family

  _____

3. entered the harbor

  _____

4. everyone on shore

  _____

5. ate Korean food for dinner

  _____

 **Work with a partner. Pick one group of words from above. Think
of as many complete sentences as you can.**

Name _____   Date _____

Map and Talk

Use a Venn diagram to compare and contrast a day at school with a day at home.

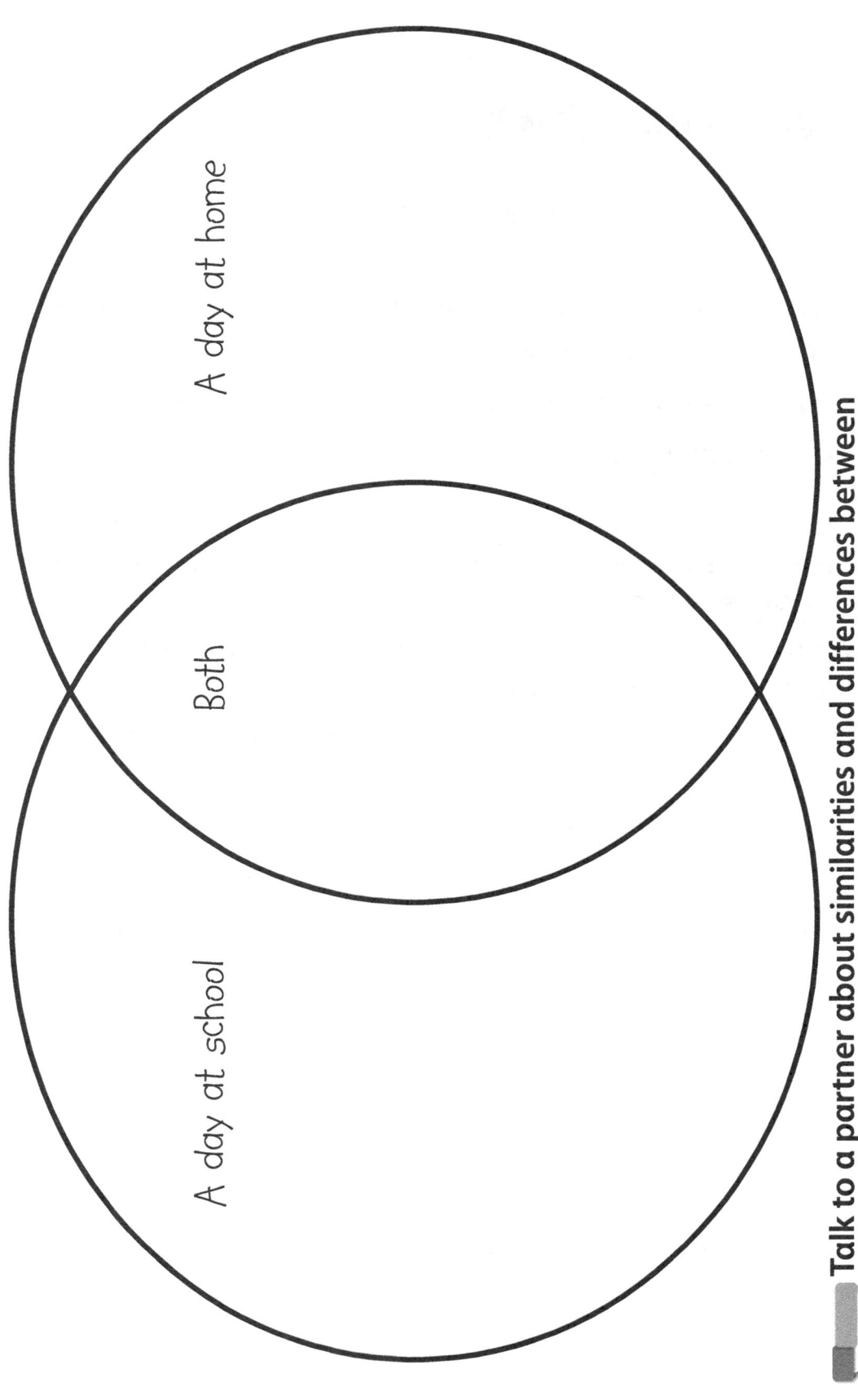

A day at home

Both

A day at school

Talk to a partner about similarities and differences between a day at school and a day at home.

Grammar

Two into One

Grammar Rules Compound Subjects

1. When *and* joins <u>**two simple subjects**</u>, use a **verb** that tells about more than one.

2. When *or* joins <u>**two subjects**</u>, use a **verb** that agrees with the <u>**simple subject**</u> closest to it.

1. Find sentences with the same <u>predicate</u>. Jen <u>bakes bread.</u> Ed <u>bakes bread.</u>

2. Write a new sentence with a <u>compound subject.</u> <u>Jen and Ed</u> bake bread.

3. Make sure your new subject agrees with the verb.

Tim makes great tacos.	Bill makes great tacos.	Lan arrives at the party first.	My mother cooks family dinners.
Jimmy buys spices at the store.	My father cooks family dinners.	Lin buys spices at the store.	Sara arrives at the party first.

_____

_____

_____

_____

Name _____ Date _____

"A Writer's Journey"

Listen as your teacher reads. Follow with your finger.

1

Xiaolu Guo lived with her grandparents in Shitang, a fishing village in the southeastern region of China. Xiaolu enjoyed talking to the stationmaster. He told her stories about China and about heroes who traveled to distant places. Xiaolu longed to explore the world one day.

2

As she grew up, Xiaolu started to write her own books and make her own films. When she was in her twenties, she went to study at the National Film and Television School in England. At first, Xiaolu found it hard to settle in. She did not know anyone, and she found English difficult.

3

Xiaolu moved to London. She made new friends and loved the cultural diversity in the city. She realized that many people, just like her, were learning English, too. The first book she published was about a young woman from China who was living in London and learning English. Xiaolu wrote more books and won several awards.

Grammar

The Life of Xiaolu Guo

Grammar Rule Compound Predicates

A **compound predicate** has two or more **verbs** joined by *and* or *or*.

Combine the sentences to write one longer sentence.

1. He would tell her stories about ancient China. He would tell her stories about warriors and heroes.

   _____

2. Xiaolu left China. Xiaolu traveled to England to study.

   _____

3. Xiaolu thought people in England were rich. Xiaolu thought people in England were well dressed.

   _____

4. In London, Xiaolu wasn't lonely. In London, Xiaolu wasn't unhappy.

   _____

5. Xiaolu wrote books in English. Xiaolu received many awards.

   _____

 **Write two sentences with the same subject. Use a different verb in each sentence. Have a partner combine the sentences into one sentence that has a compound predicate.**

© Cengage Learning, Inc.

Vocabulary

Words Around the World

Play a game using Key Words.

1. The traveler stands behind a challenger.

2. The challenger listens to the traveler's clue and names the Key Word.

3. The traveler moves behind the next student on the right if the challenger answers correctly. The first traveler to go all around the circle wins.

KEY WORDS

citizenship	customs	identity	adapt	origin

CLUES

- where you come from
- who you are
- traditions
- being a citizen
- to change

© Cengage Learning, Inc.

Reread and Retell

"A Writer's Journey"

Complete a Venn diagram for "A Writer's Journey."

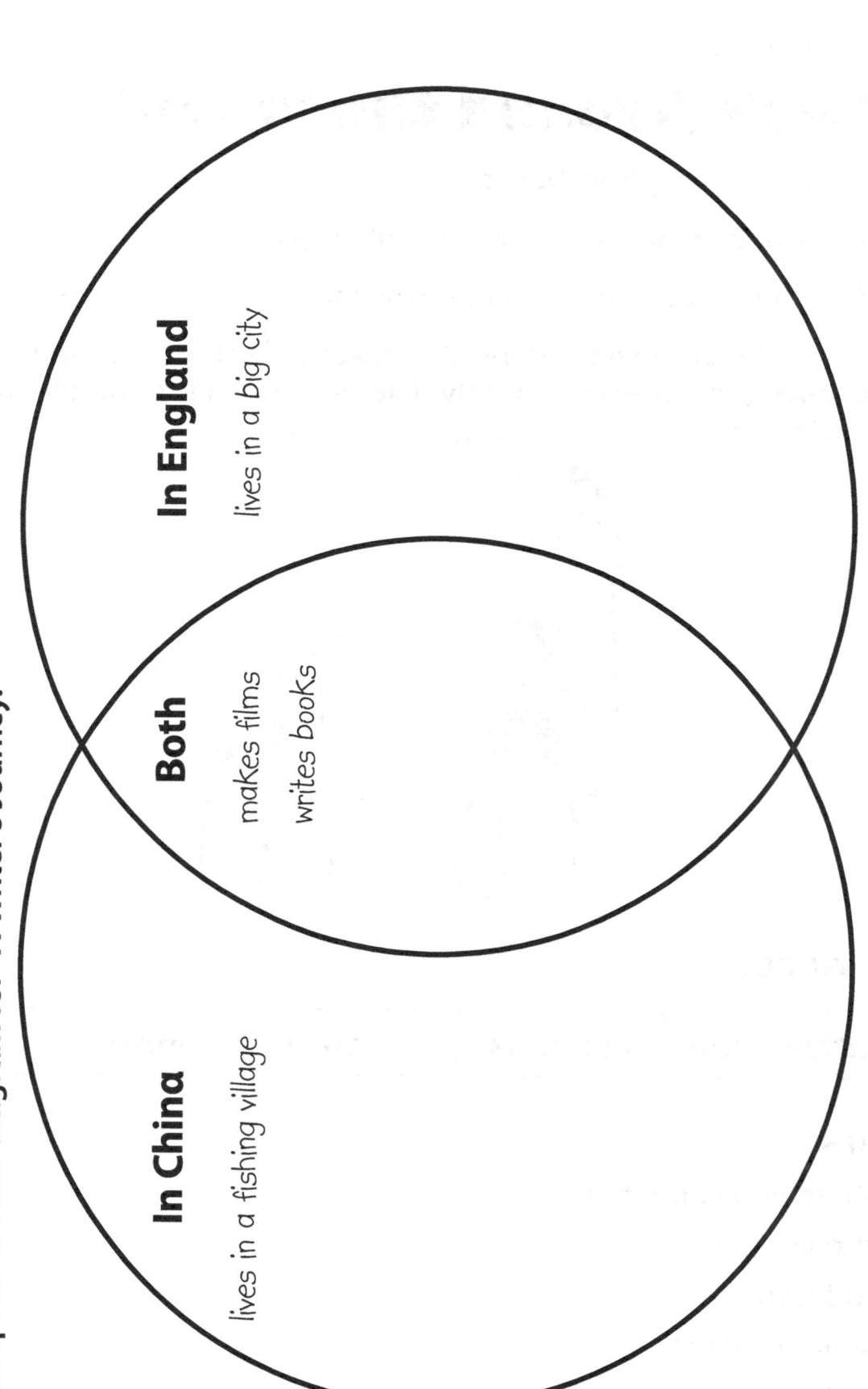

In China

lives in a fishing village

Both

makes films

writes books

In England

lives in a big city

➤ **Use the Venn diagram to tell a partner how life was the same for Xiaolu Guo in each place.**

© Cengage Learning, Inc.

Fluency

"A Writer's Journey"

Use this passage to practice reading with proper expression.

Xiaolu grew older and began to write books and make films.	11
When she was in her late twenties, she applied for a scholarship to	24
study in England. More than 500 people applied for the scholarship.	35
One day, Xiaolu received a phone call from Beijing.	44
"Congratulations! You have won a scholarship!" she was told.	53
The scholarship would pay for her to study at the National Film	65
and Television School in England.	70
Xiaolu prepared to travel to England. She imagined that she	80
would smell the breezes brought by the Atlantic Ocean and walk	91
through gentle rains.	94
Her mother was worried. "They don't know how to cook rice in	106
the West!" she said. "What will you eat?"	114

From "A Writer's Journey," page 49

Expression

B ☐ Does not read with feeling.   A ☐ Reads with appropriate feeling for most content.

I ☐ Reads with some feeling, but does not match content.   AH ☐ Reads with appropriate feeling for all content.

Accuracy and Rate Formula

Use the formula to measure a reader's accuracy and rate while reading aloud.

_____	–	_____	=	_____
words attempted in one minute		number of errors		words correct per minute (wcpm)

"Migrant Stories from Around the World"

Complete this dialogue journal as you read "Migrant Stories from Around the World."

What I think	What my partner thinks
Page _____ _____ _____	_____ _____ _____
Page _____ _____ _____	_____ _____ _____
Page _____ _____ _____	_____ _____ _____
Page _____ _____ _____	_____ _____ _____

Tell a partner your thoughts about each page. Then ask a partner to share his or her thoughts.

Respond and Extend

Compare Literary Language

Use a chart to compare literary language in "A Writer's Journey" and "Migrant Stories from Around the World."

	"A Writer's Journey"	"Migrant Stories from Around the World"
People		"It's hard to get close to people, but once you do, the friendship is forever," she says.
Events		
Places	Instead of big, beautiful houses, she saw short, gray buildings against the dark sky.	

Take turns with a partner. Compare the literary language used in both selections.

Grammar

Grammar Rules Compound Subjects

1. When *and* joins **two simple subjects**, use a **verb** that tells about more than one.
2. When *or* joins **two subjects**, use a **verb** that agrees with the **simple subject** closest to it.

Read each pair of sentences. Combine the subjects into a compound subject and write the new sentence. Be sure your subject agrees with the verb.

1. Mom goes to the city. Dad goes to the city.

   _____

2. The train brings them downtown. The bus brings them downtown.

   _____

3. The grocery store is open. The bakery is open.

   _____

4. The vegetables are fresh. The bread is fresh.

   _____

Write two sentences with a different subject. Have a partner combine them into one sentence with a compound subject.

© Cengage Learning, Inc.

Name _____   Date _____

Ideas

Writing is well-developed when the message is clear and interesting to the reader. It is supported by details that show the writer knows the topic well.

	Is the message clear and interesting?	**Do the details show the writer knows the topic?**
4 Wow!	❏ All the writing is clear and focused. ❏ The writing is very interesting.	❏ All the details are about the topic. The writer knows the topic well.
3 Ahh.	❏ Most of the writing is clear and focused. ❏ Most of the writing is interesting.	❏ Most of the details are about the topic. The writer knows the topic fairly well.
2 Hmm.	❏ Some of the writing is not clear. The writing lacks some focus. ❏ Some of the writing is confusing.	❏ Some details are about the topic. The writer doesn't know the topic well.
1 Huh?	❏ The writing is not clear or focused. ❏ The writing is confusing.	❏ Many details are not about the topic. The writer does not know the topic.

Writing Project

T-Chart

Write your topic. Then write details in the chart about a time you had to adjust to a new situation or place.

Central Topic: _____

Setting 1: _____	Setting 2: _____

Writing Project

Revise

Use revision marks to make changes to this paragraph. Look for:

- **relevant details**
- **concluding sentence**

Revision Marks	
∧	Add
℘	Delete
⏋	Indent

The plaza in my town in mexico has many food sellers.

There are mountains nearby. Farmers cell fruit and vegetables. Fish

sellers bring the fish they have caught to market in buckets and

large bins. I like watching the surfers on the beach.

Sometimes the fish sellers will cook the fish for you. I like fish tacos

the best. The bus can take you to the city if you want to go there.

Fish tacos melt in your mouth.

Edit and Proofread

Use revision marks to edit and
proofread this paragraph. Look for:

- compound subject-verb
  agreement
- end marks
- compound words: regular and
  hyphenated

Revision Marks	
∧	Add
℘	Delete
⌣	Close up

The fruit stall and fish stands is open at different times. The stalls

selling clothes and other goods stays open until 8:00 P.M. The stalls

with fruit, vegetables, and shell fish close by 4:00 P.M. If you want

fresh food, it is best to get there early

Unit Concept Map

Catching the Light

Make a concept map with the answers to the Big Question:
What is the power of the sun?

What is
the power
of the sun?

Name _____   Date _____

Our Characters

Choose a story with a conflict and complete a character chart.

Character	Role	Function	Conflict

Grammar

The Fantastic Sun

Grammar Rules Kinds of Sentences

1. Use a **statement** to say something.
2. Use a **command** to tell someone to do something.
3. Use an **exclamation** to show strong feeling. End it with an exclamation point. (!)
4. Use a **negative sentence** to say "No" about something.
5. Use contractions to make two words into one word: **can't won't**, **don't**, **doesn't**, **isn't**, **aren't**.

Label each sentence to show what type it is. Circle any contractions.

1. The sun is fantastic! _____

2. I want to learn about the sun. _____

3. Get your coat. _____

4. I don't need a coat inside. _____

5. You can't learn about the sun here. _____

6. We will go to the library. _____

Tell a partner something about the sun. Use at least two kinds of sentences and one contraction.

Name _____   Date _____

"Ten Suns"

Listen as your teacher reads. Follow with your finger.

1

Long ago, there were ten suns, the children of Di Jun and his wife, Xi He. Each day, one of the suns walked across the sky, bringing warmth and light.

2

The suns were tired of following the same path across the sky alone. They decided to walk together. The heat of the ten suns began to burn Earth.

3

Di Jun and Xi He called for their sons to come back, but they did not listen. Di Jun did not want Earth destroyed, so he had the Archer of Heaven shoot down the suns. As each boy was hit by an arrow, he turned into a crow.

4

Di Jun realized that if all the suns were destroyed, Earth would be plunged into icy darkness. He left just one sun to heat Earth.

Grammar

The Question Game

Grammar Rules Questions: *Do/Does; Yes/No* Answers

1. A **question** ends with a question mark.
2. A **question** can begin with the word **Do** or **Does**.
3. You may answer a question using **yes** or **no** and, if you wish, a contraction. For example: *No, I do not.* or *No, I don't.*

Unscramble the words to ask a question. Then answer your question.

1. crows / Do / fly / ? _____

_____

2. shine / the / sun / Does / ? _____

_____

3. have / ten / Do / suns / we / ? _____

_____

4. Does / a / sunlight / plant / absorb / ? _____

_____

5. need / animals / Do / sunlight / ? _____

_____

6. into / people / suns / turn / Do / ? _____

_____

Name _____ Date _____

"Ten Suns"

Complete the chart about the characters in "Ten Suns."

Character	Role	Function	Conflict
Di Jun	father		His sons want to light the sky all at once.
ten suns			

Use your chart to retell the myth to a partner.

Fluency

"Ten Suns"

Use this passage to practice reading with proper intonation.

Hou Yi refused. "How can I harm your boys? They are like my   13

children. I taught them to shoot with a bow and arrow. We both still   27

love them, even when they disobey."   33

"I love the creatures of Earth, too. I must protect them," Di Jun   46

told Hou Yi. "Do not be afraid. You will not harm the boys. My sons   61

will not be hurt, but they will be changed. Never again will they cross   75

the sky as suns. They will be gods no more. Hurry! Do as I command.   90

There is no time to spare. Earth is dying."   99

From "Ten Suns," page 94

Intonation

B ☐ Does not change pitch.	**A** ☐ Changes pitch to match some of the content.
I ☐ Changes pitch, but does not match content.	**AH** ☐ Changes pitch to match all the content.

Accuracy and Rate Formula

Use the formula to measure a reader's accuracy and rate while reading aloud.

_____   −   _____   =   _____
words attempted   number of errors   words correct per minute
in one minute   (wcpm)

Name _____ Date _____

"How the Fifth Sun Came to Be"

Complete this reflection journal as you read the origin myth.

Page	My question	The answer

How did you figure out the answers to your questions? Tell a partner.

Name _____ Date _____

Respond and Extend

Compare Myths

Use the comparison chart to compare the myths.

	"Ten Suns"	"How the Fifth Sun Came to Be"
The type of myth		Aztec
What the myth explains		
Setting		Mexico
The characters	**Gods:** **Heroes:** **Other:**	**Gods:** **Heroes:** **Other:**
What the story is about	**Beginning:** **Middle:** **End:**	**Beginning:** **Middle:** **End:**
The story's message		

Take turns with a partner. Share another message you think each myth has.

© Cengage Learning, Inc.

Grammar

The Story of the Sun

Grammar Rules Kinds of Sentences

1. Use a **statement** to tell something.
2. Use a **command** to tell someone to do something.
3. Use an **exclamation** to show strong feeling. End it with an exclamation point. (!)
4. Use a **question** to ask something. End it with a question mark. (?)

Follow the directions. Use a contraction in at least one sentence.

1. Write a statement about the sun's power.

_____

2. Write an exclamation about the sun.

_____

3. Write a question you have about the sun.

_____

4. Write a command about staying safe in the sun.

_____

Listen as a partner tells you something about the sun. Use a different kind of sentence to respond.

© Cengage Learning, Inc.

Thinking Map

A School Project

Complete a goal-and-outcome chart about a problem in your school.

Goal		Obstacles		Strategies		Outcome
	→		→		→	

Use your chart to tell a partner about the goal and how it was achieved.

Grammar

Energy for Our Planet

Grammar Rules Compound Sentences

A **compound sentence** joins ideas with a **comma** plus a **conjunction**.

- Use **and** to join ideas that are alike.
- Use **but** to join ideas that are different.
- Use **or** to join ideas that show a choice.
- Use **so** to explain why.

Create a compound sentence from each pair of sentences.

1. Solar energy is powerful. Not enough people use its power.

_____

_____

2. Solar cells capture the sunlight. They use the light energy to

create electricity. _____

_____

3. Electrical power plants can get energy from coal. They can get

it from oil. _____

_____

Tell a partner what you know about the sun. Have a partner tell you an idea, too. Combine your ideas into a compound sentence.

Name _____   Date _____

"Energy for the Future"

Listen as your teacher reads. Follow with your finger.

Thomas Culhane teaches people about solar power. Very few people around the world use solar power, and he wants to change that.

Culhane went to Cairo, Egypt, to teach students how to use the sun's energy to make hot water. The students learned that there are many types of energy, including chemical energy, electrical energy, and light energy. Solar-powered water heaters use the sun's energy.

COLD WATER FLOWS TO THE BOTTOM OF THE PIPES

BLACK ALUMINUM FINS ABSORB HEAT AND TRANSFER IT TO THE PIPES

AS THE WATER WARMS, IT RISES THROUGH THE PIPES TO THE TOP OF THE TANK

The students built a water heater with large, black panels to absorb the sun's energy. That energy becomes the heat that warms the water pipes inside the panels. As the water inside the pipes gets warmer, it rises and moves through the pipes to a storage tank. A pipe carries the hot water down to the schoolyard. Culhane told the students, "This is just the beginning!"

Grammar

Use Complex Sentences

Grammar Rule Compound and Complex Sentences

A **complex sentence** has one **independent clause**, or main clause, and at least one **dependent clause**.

Expand each independent clause by using the conjunction in parentheses to create a complex sentence. Say each sentence.

1. We can't understand the sun's importance _____

_____ (if)

2. I am surprised when it rains _____

_____ (because)

3. I don't need to plug in my solar calculator _____

_____ (since)

4. Chemical reactions occur inside my body _____

_____ (after)

5. Atoms inside solar cells release electrons _____

_____ (when)

Reread and Retell

"Energy for the Future"

Reread "Energy for the Future" and complete the goal-and-outcome chart.

Goal	Obstacles	Strategies	Outcome
to use the sun's energy to heat water			

Use your chart to retell the selection to a partner.

Name _____ Date _____

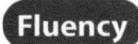

"Energy for the Future"

Use this passage to practice reading with proper phrasing.

Today we had a problem. We tested our metal storage tank. It leaked!   13

Then one student had an idea. He took me to a place where plastic   27

barrels from a shampoo factory were being resold. The barrels were   38

inexpensive and perfect for our hot water heaters.   46

When we returned, the students cheered. "But how will the water in the   59

tank stay hot?" asked one student. "Maybe it just needs a blanket," said   72

another.   73

Clearly, the students have become energy problem-solvers. At the end   84

of the day today, we insulated our tank with a "blanket" of fiberglass   97

insulation and then gave each other high-fives.   105

From "Energy for the Future," page 132

Phrasing

☐ ☐ Rarely pauses while reading the text.   ☐ ☐ Frequently pauses at appropriate points in the text.

☐ ☐ Occasionally pauses while reading the text.   ☐ ☐ Consistently pauses at all appropriate points in the text.

Accuracy and Rate Formula

Use the formula to measure a reader's accuracy and rate while reading aloud.

_____ − _____ = _____
words attempted   number of errors   words correct per minute
in one minute   (wcpm)

Name _____ Date _____

"How to Make a Solar Oven"

Complete this reflection journal as you read the how-to article.

Page	My question	The answer

How did you figure out the answers to your questions?

_____

Name _____ Date _____

Compare Online Documents

Use the chart to compare online documents.

	"How to Make a Solar Oven"	"Energy for the Future"
Genre		
Point of View	first person ☐ second person ☐ third person ☐	first person ☐ second person ☐ third person ☐
Formal or Informal **1.** Analyze the writing. **2.** Check the boxes that describe the writing. **3.** Decide if the writing is formal or informal.	Did the writer use: slang ☐ exclamation points ☐ abbreviations ☐ questions ☐ conversational voice ☐ formal ☐ informal ☐	Did the writer use: slang ☐ exclamation points ☐ abbreviations ☐ questions ☐ conversational voice ☐ formal ☐ informal ☐

 Talk with a partner about how the purpose of a blog is different from that of a how-to article.

© Cengage Learning, Inc.

Grammar

Sun-Baked Potatoes

Grammar Rules Compound and Complex Sentences

1. To make a **compound sentence**, use a <u>**comma**</u> and a <u>**conjunction**</u> (<u>**and**</u>, <u>**but**</u>, <u>**or**</u>, <u>**so**</u>, <u>**yet**</u>, or <u>**nor**</u>) to join two **independent clauses**.

2. Join a **dependent clause** with an **independent clause** to make a **complex sentence**. Use a <u>**comma**</u> if the **dependent clause** comes first. Use words such as **when**, **because**, **although**, **while**, and **since**.

Write compound and complex sentences.

_____ you can bake potatoes in an electric or gas oven, it's fun to bake them in the sun! A solar oven may be small _____ it does work. First, wash the potatoes _____ then put them in a pot. The pot must be black _____ it will not absorb enough heat from the sun to cook the potatoes. _____ your potatoes bake, have fun. The food won't burn _____ your potatoes will take about six hours to bake.

▬▬▬ Write one compound and one complex sentence and share them with a partner.

Name _____ Date _____

Ideas

Writing is well-developed when the message is clear and interesting to the reader. It is supported by details that show the writer knows the topic well.

	Is the message clear and interesting?	**Do the details show the writer knows the topic?**
4 Wow!	❑ All the writing is clear and focused. ❑ The writing is very interesting.	❑ All the details are about the topic. The writer knows the topic well.
3 Ahh.	❑ Most of the writing is clear and focused. ❑ Most of the writing is interesting.	❑ Most of the details are about the topic. The writer knows the topic fairly well.
2 Hmm.	❑ Some of the writing is not clear. The writing lacks some focus. ❑ Some of the writing is confusing.	❑ Some details are about the topic. The writer doesn't know the topic well.
1 Huh?	❑ The writing is not clear or focused. ❑ The writing is confusing.	❑ Many details are not about the topic. The writer does not know the topic.

Name _____   Date _____

Writing Project

Character Chart

Complete the character chart for your myth.

Character	Role	Function	Conflict

Writing Project

Revise

Use revision marks to make changes to these paragraphs. Look for:

- **details that help develop the main idea**
- **varied sentence types**

	Revision Marks	
∧	Add
ℒ	Take out
∧̣	Add a comma
∧!	Add an exclamation point
∧?	Add a question mark

Why Do We Have Tornados?

the world was young. Wolf and Rabbit were friends. Snake ate Rat. They did things together. they helped each other. Bananas are yellow.

They got into an argument one day. Crow flew away. Wolf said he was better. Rabbit said he was better. Wolf started to chase Rabbit.

Name _____ Date _____

Edit and Proofread

Use revision marks to edit and proofread these paragraphs.
Look for:

- **different sentence types**
- **commas in compound and complex sentences**
- **correct spelling of contractions**

Revision Marks	
∧	Add
℘	Take out
⬭ SP	Check spelling
∧̬	Add a comma
ˬ∧	Add an apostrophe
≡	Capitalize

Why Do We Have Tornados? (continued)

Wolf chased Rabbit for days on end. finally Rabbit began to tire. and He realized that Wolf would eventually catch him. "I must think of a clever trick," thought Rabbit.

Rabbit suddenly stopped. and as Wolf ran past Rabbit grabbed Wolf's tail as hard as he could. He wouldnt let go.

"Ive got him now!" laughed Wolf as he twisted around to nip at Rabbit. But no matter how far he twisted or how hard he tried Wolf couldnt quite reach Rabbit. they spun faster and faster until they stirred up a twisting wind. The wind blew so hard that it swept up rocks bushes and trees. Today we call this twisting wind a tornado. So when you hear about or see a tornado you know that Wolf is chasing Rabbit.

Unit Concept Map

Nature's Webs

Make a concept map with the answers to the Big Question:
How are animals and plants dependent on one another?

How are animals and plants dependent on one another?

Thinking Map

Retell a Story

Make a plot diagram to retell an animal story you know or have experienced.

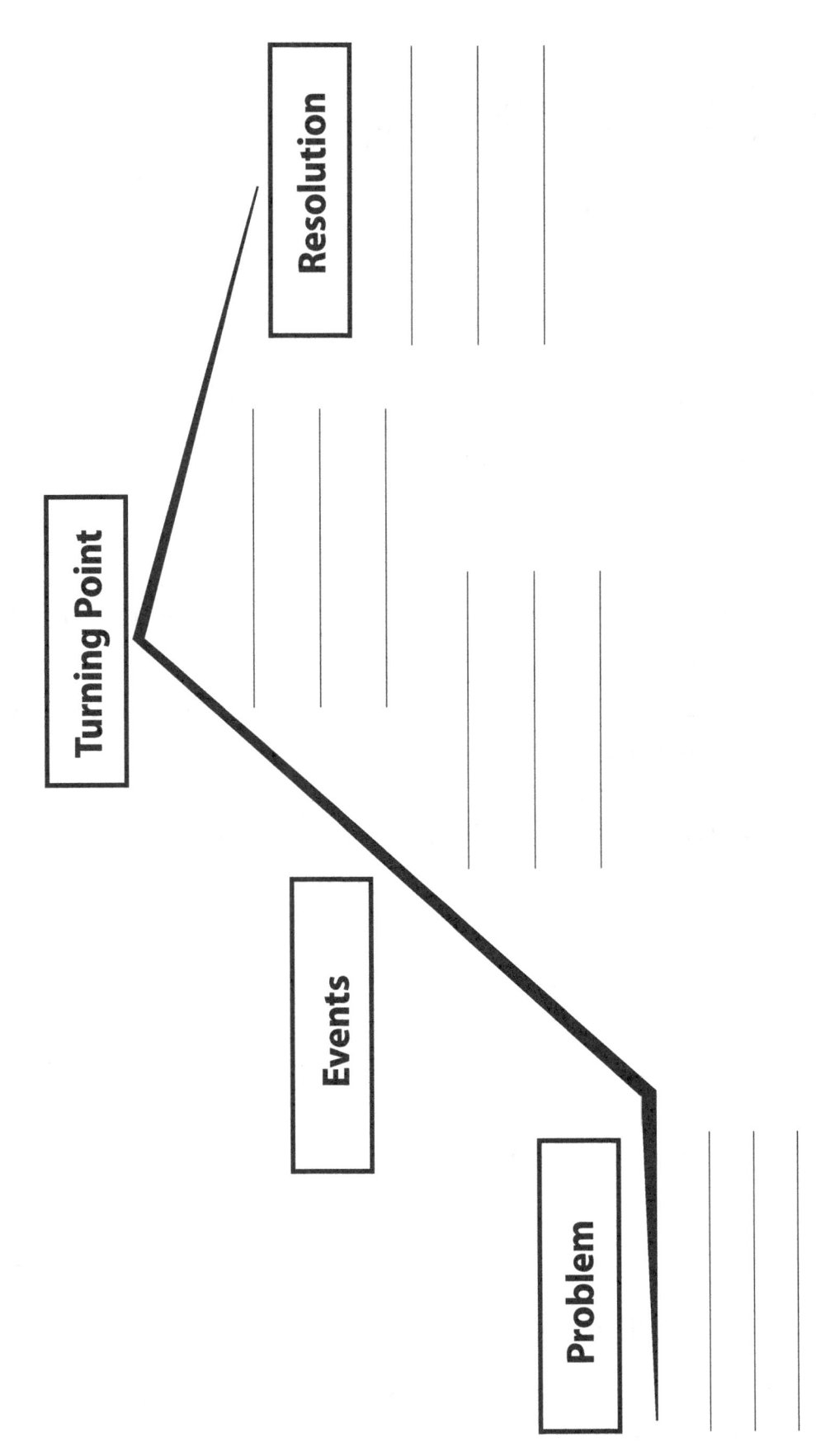

Resolution

Turning Point

Events

Problem

Retell your story. Use this plot diagram to help you.

Grammar

What's for Dinner?

Grammar Rules Nouns

A **noun** names a person or an animal, a place, a thing, or an idea.

Person or Animal	Place	Thing	Idea
owl	desert	sun	hunger

Categorize the nouns.

A <u>deer</u> searches for <u>food</u> in the <u>woods</u>. The deer snacks on tasty <u>twigs</u> and <u>blackberries</u>. A nearby <u>rabbit</u> feeds on tall <u>grass</u>. Since both deer and rabbits are <u>herbivores</u>, they can live in <u>harmony</u>. But what about other <u>animals</u> in the <u>forest</u>?

People or Animals	**Places**	**Things**	**Ideas**
deer			

Write a or an in front of each noun.

_____ bird   _____ ant   _____ idea

_____ consumer   _____ egg   _____ plant

 Tell a partner three things you have learned about nature's webs. Identify the nouns you use.

© Cengage Learning, Inc.

Name _____ Date _____

"Coyote and Badger"

Listen as your teacher reads. Follow with your finger.

There was a drought in Chaco Canyon. All the animals were hungry, even Coyote. He tried to hunt for prey, but he was too slow.

Badger and her pups were also hungry. Badger dug many holes to try to catch her prey, but she went home hungry, too.

One night, Coyote heard Badger digging. A rat ran out of its hole. Coyote caught it. Another rat came up and saw Coyote. It went back down the hole. Badger caught it.

Outside the hole, Badger and Coyote sniffed and growled at each other. Then they relaxed. They formed a partnership and began hunting together. It was much better than hunting alone.

The drought got worse. Coyote and Badger had to travel far to find food. One night, an eagle killed one of Badger's pups. Badger and her other pup went away.

Coyote had to hunt alone again. Then the rains came. There would be more food for all the animals.

Grammar

The Make-It-Plural Game

Grammar Rules Plural Nouns

1. A **noun** names a person or an animal, a place, a thing, or an idea.

2. Add **-s** to form the plural of most nouns.

3. Add **-es** to form the plural of nouns that end in
   x, **ch**, **sh**, **ss**, **z**, and sometimes **o**.

1. Play with a partner.

2. Spin the spinner.

3. Change the noun to a plural noun. Say a sentence that includes the plural noun.

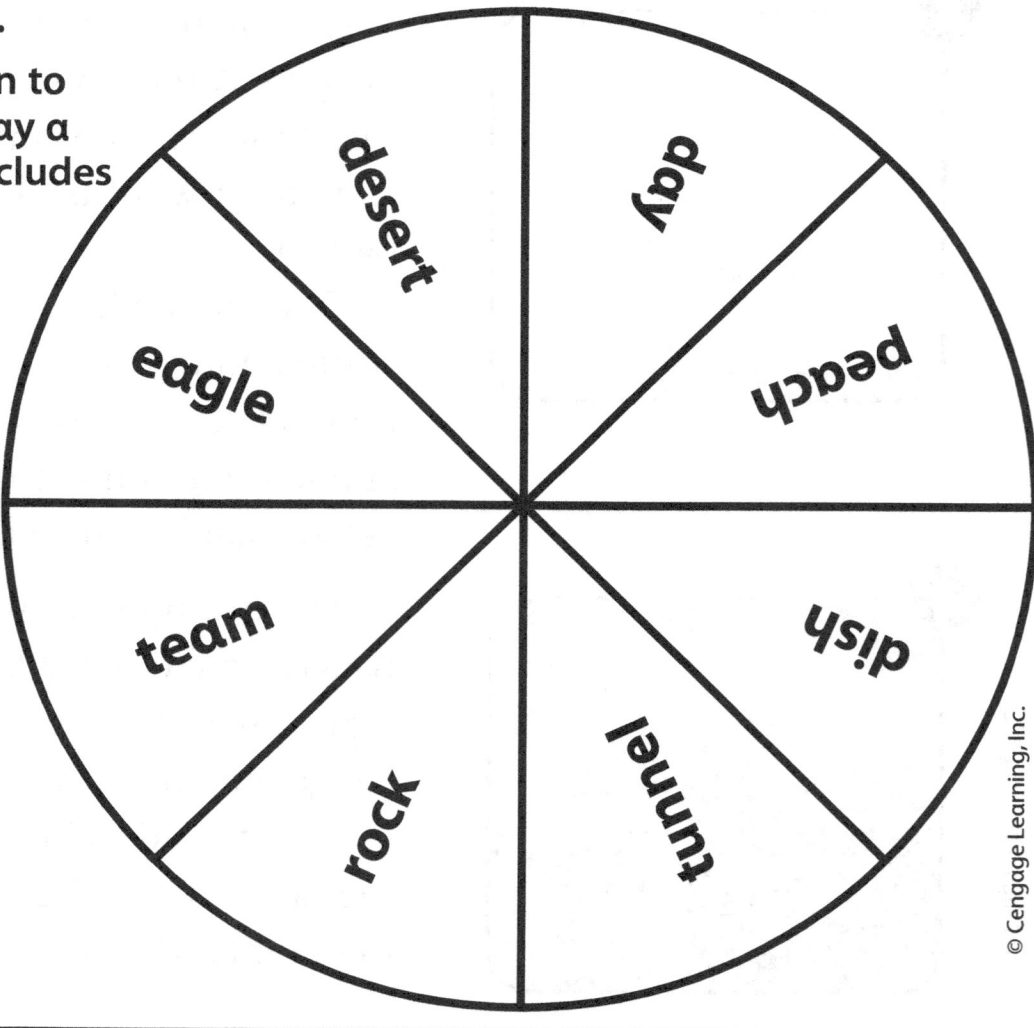

Make a Spinner

1. Place one loop of a paper clip over the center of the circle.

2. Push a sharp pencil through the loop and the paper.

3. Spin the paper clip around the pencil.

© Cengage Learning, Inc.

Vocabulary Bingo

Play Bingo using the Key Words from this unit.

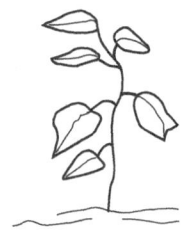

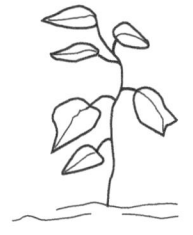

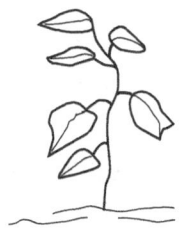

Name _____   Date _____

"Coyote and Badger"

Make a plot diagram for "Coyote and Badger."

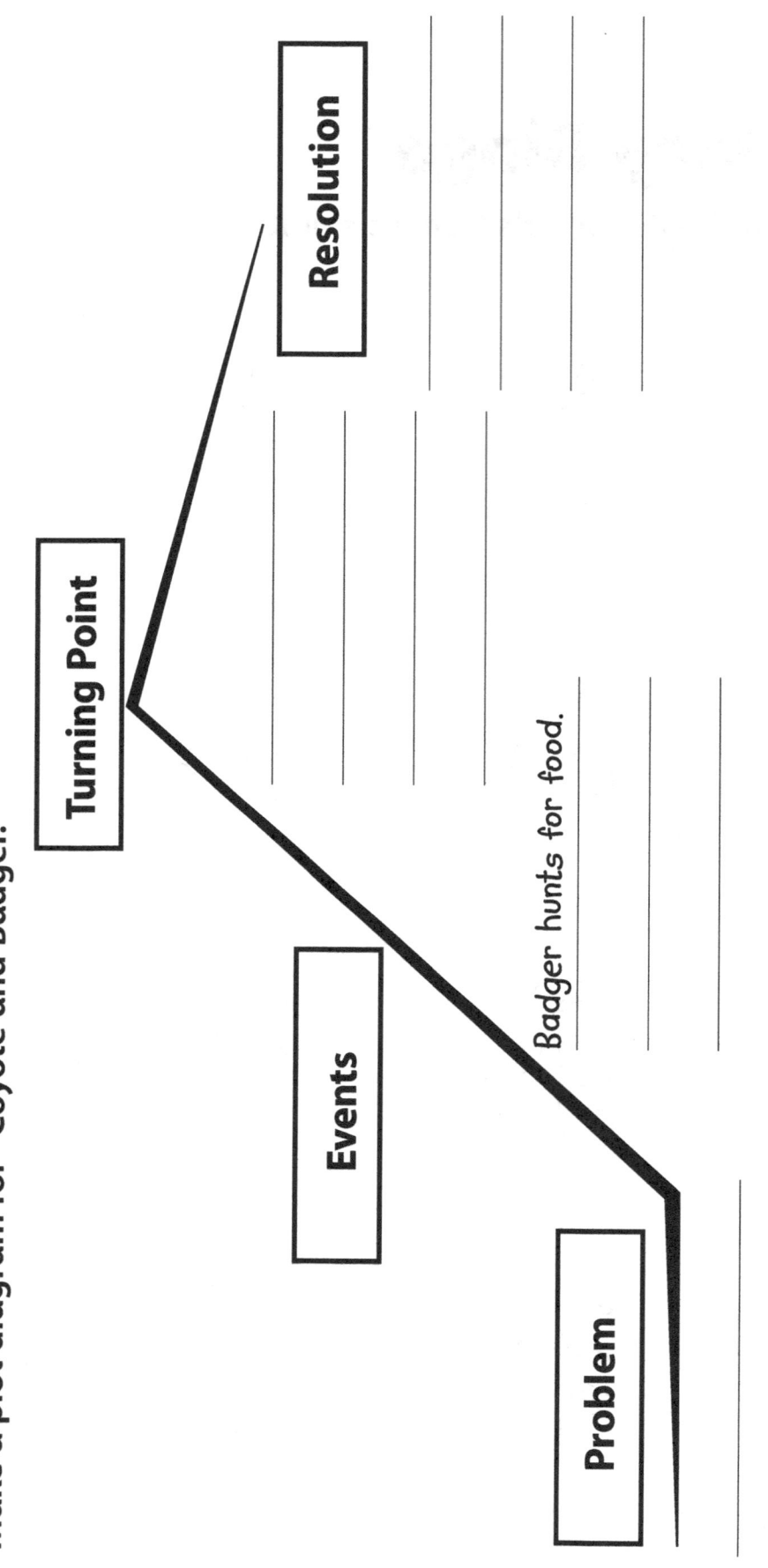

Turning Point

Resolution

Events

Badger hunts for food.

Problem

Use your plot diagram to retell the story to a partner.

3.7

Name _____ Date _____

"Coyote and Badger"

Use this passage to practice reading with proper intonation.

Farther up the canyon, Badger emerged from her den. She left her	12
two pups safely underground and waddled off as the air began to cool.	25
Badger was a night hunter, too, but she seldom chased rabbits. She was	38
a digger, not a runner.	43
When Badger found the hole of an antelope squirrel, she tore into	55
the hard soil with her long claws. The dirt flew, and in a wink, she was	71
underground following a dark tunnel. No animal can dig as fast as	83
a badger, but the squirrel raced ahead and escaped.	92

From "Coyote and Badger," page 162

Intonation

B ☐ Does not change pitch.	**A** ☐ Changes pitch to match some of the content.
I ☐ Changes pitch, but does not match content.	**AH** ☐ Changes pitch to match all the content.

Accuracy and Rate Formula

Use the formula to measure a reader's accuracy and rate while reading aloud.

_____ − _____ = _____
words attempted   number of errors   words correct per minute
in one minute   (wcpm)

Name _____ Date _____

"Living Links"

Complete the K-W-L-Q chart as you read the expository nonfiction.

K What I know	W What I want to learn	L What I learned	Q Questions I still have

Share your questions with a partner. Try to answer the questions together.

Name _____   Date _____

Compare Content

Add the names of plants and animals from "Coyote and Badger" to the correct places in this food web.

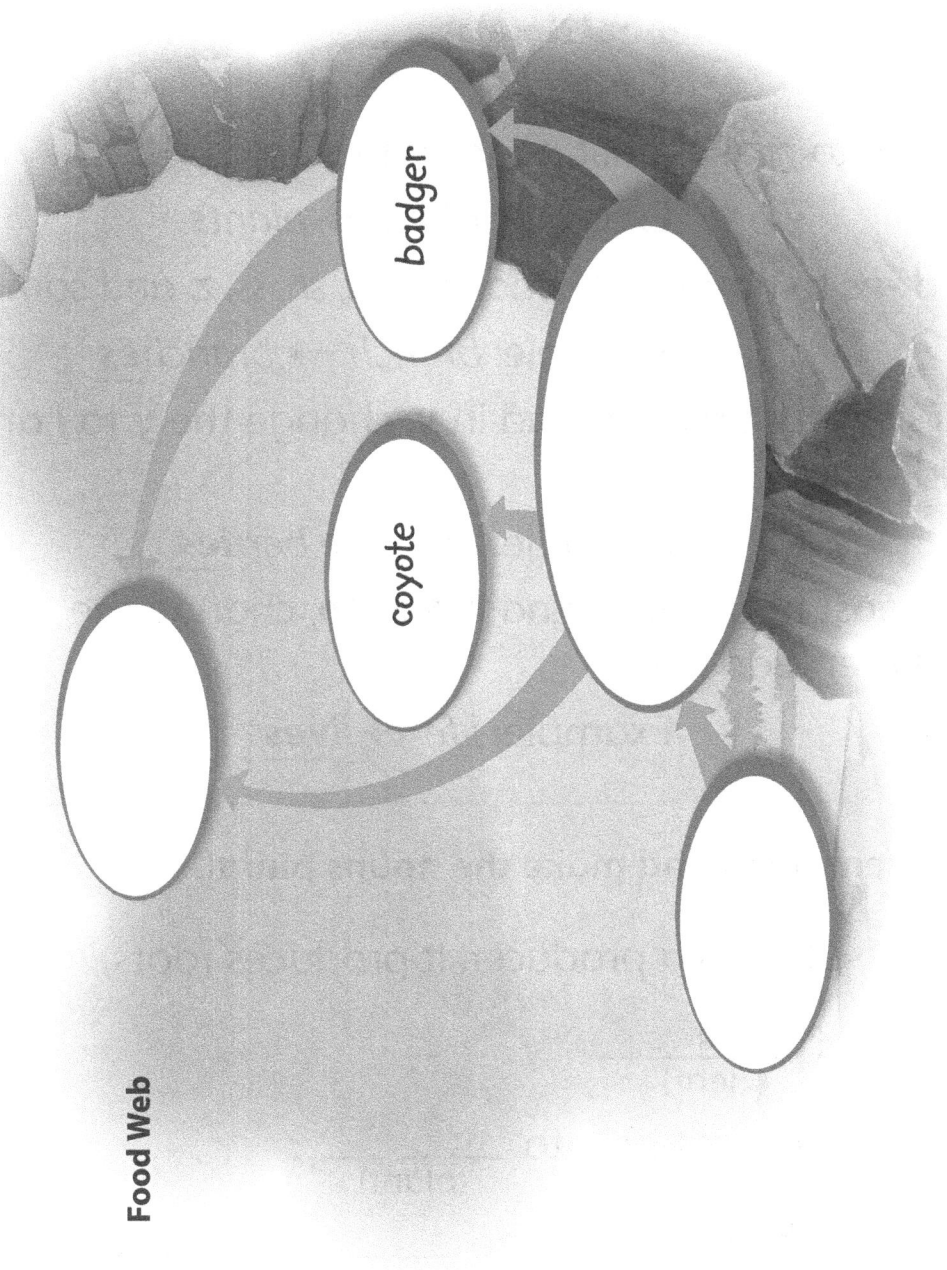

Food Web

(within diagram: badger, coyote)

Talk to a partner about how the animals and plants in this food web are connected.

Grammar

What Do They Eat?

Grammar Rules Plural Nouns

1. Add **-s** to make most nouns plural.

   Example: *plant* → *plant**s***

2. Add **-es** to nouns that end in *x, ch, sh, ss, z,* and sometimes *o.*

   Example: *branch* → *branch**es***

3. For most nouns that end in **y**, change the **y** to **i** and then add **-es**.

   Example: *berry* → *berr**ies***

4. For most nouns that end in **f** or **fe**, change the **f** or **fe** to **v** and then add **-es**.

   Example: *life* → *li**ves***

Read the sentences and make the nouns plural.

1. A potato plant is a producer. It produces roots,

   stems, and ___leaves___ .
   (leaf)

2. Some animals eat potato _plants_ .
   (plant)

3. They need the energy in the _potato_ to survive.
   (potato)

4. Animals like _foxes_ also eat other animals.
   (fox)

5. Eagles sometimes eat badger _babies_ .
   (baby)

Small Things, Big Idea!

Ask a partner to think about a small plant or animal that is important. Write a main idea about it on the left side of a tree diagram. List details that support that idea on the right.

Main Idea	Details
tree help us in daily life	they give us oxegen,
	We make paper out of them.
	We make homes out of them.

Use your tree diagram to track the main idea and details a partner gives about why a small plant or animal is important.

Grammar

Living Things

Grammar Rules Count/Noncount Nouns

Nouns that you can count have a **singular form** and a **plural form**. Nouns that you cannot count have the same form for "one" and "more than one."

Count Nouns	Noncount Nouns
birds, flowers	prey, weather

Categorize the nouns.

Scientists who study biology learn about living things like plants and animals. All living things need energy. Plants use sunlight, water, and nutrients to get energy. This is known as photosynthesis. Many animals eat plants to get energy.

Count Nouns	Noncount Nouns
scientists	biology
things	energy
plants	sunlight
Animals	water
nutrients	photosynthesis

 **Use three of the nouns above. Tell a partner something about nature.**

Name _____   Date _____

"Fish of the Future"

Listen as your teacher reads. Follow with your finger.

1

Dr. Tierney Thys studies the ocean's ecosystem. She focuses on the sunfish. She believes that understanding how the ocean environment is connected is crucial for its health and our survival.

2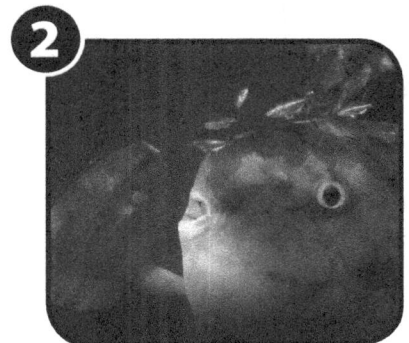

The sunfish holds three world records. As it grows, it increases in weight more than other vertebrates. It is the world's heaviest bony fish. It produces more eggs at one time than any other vertebrate.

3

Overfishing is reducing the numbers of fish. Jellyfish compete with other fish for food. Because it eats jellyfish, the sunfish may keep their population under control.

4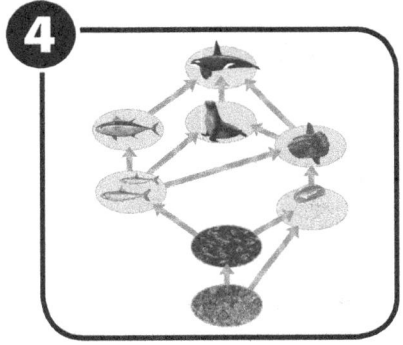

Dr. Thys says the sunfish may be the fish of the future. All creatures have a place in the world, and it's important to keep the ocean system whole.

Grammar

The Irregulars

Grammar Rules Irregular Plurals

Some words have special spellings for "more than one."

Example: *foot* ⟶ *feet*

Match each noun with its irregular plural form.

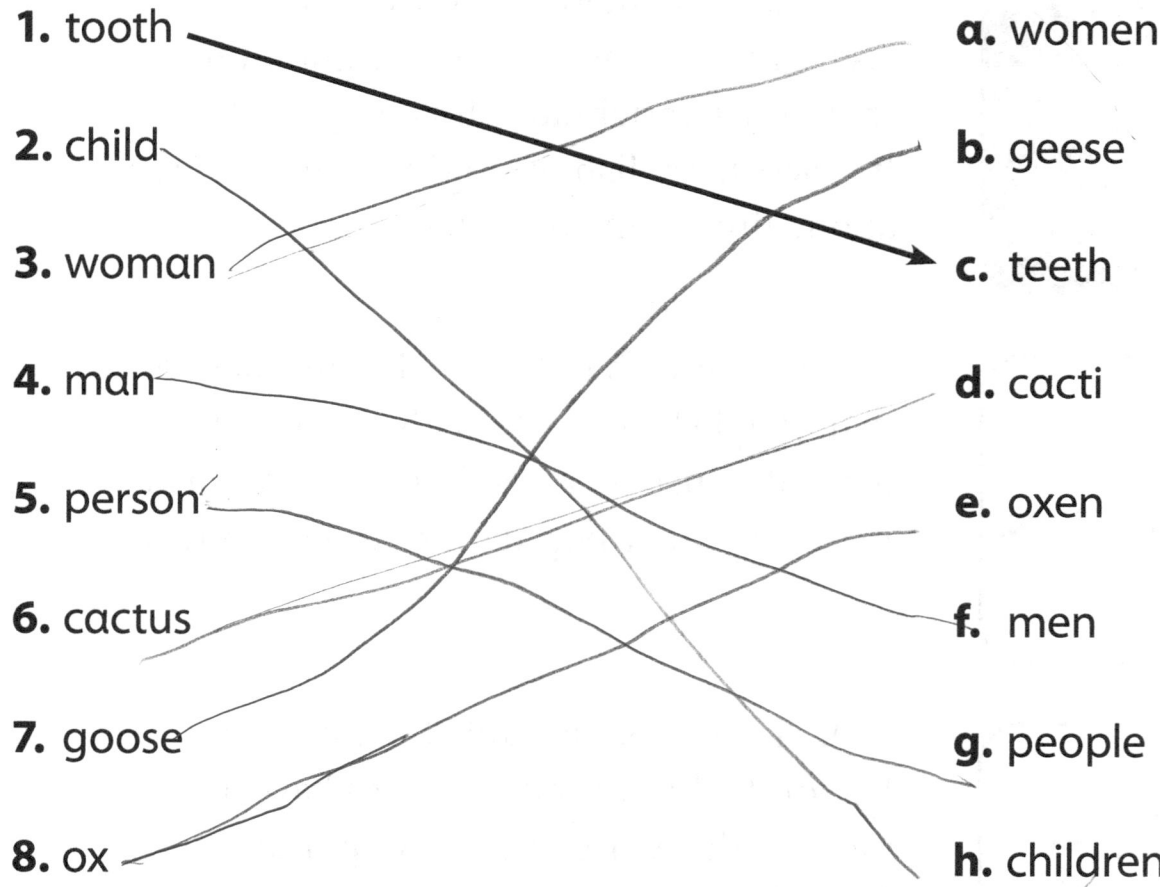

1. tooth   **a.** women

2. child   **b.** geese

3. woman   **c.** teeth

4. man   **d.** cacti

5. person   **e.** oxen

6. cactus   **f.** men

7. goose   **g.** people

8. ox   **h.** children

Use two of the irregular plural nouns above. Tell a partner something about you.

Name _____

"Fish of the Future

Reread "Fish of the Future" and fill in the ch
and details.

p. 194–197 What's special about the sunfish?	It has a strange body shape.
	It lies on its side at the ocean's surface as if it's sunning itself.
	It has a beak-like mouth.
	It is covered with parasites.

Use your tree diagram to summarize the interview for a partner.

...ure"

...ading with proper expression.

...e world records! As it grows, it increases in	12
...t more than any other vertebrate—up to 60 million times its size at	26
hatching. If you grew that much, you'd be as big as 30 thousand school buses!	41
Second, it is the world's heaviest bony fish. The heaviest sunfish ever recorded	54
weighed more than 2,300 kilograms (over 5,000 pounds). That's as heavy	65
as ten grand pianos, or five large cows!	73
Third, the sunfish produces more eggs at one time than any other vertebrate.	86
Scientists found one mother sunfish carrying an estimated 300 million eggs.	97

From "Fish of the Future," page 196

Expression

B ☐ Does not read with feeling.

I ☐ Reads with some feeling, but does not match content.

A ☐ Reads with appropriate feeling for most content.

AH ☐ Reads with appropriate feeling for all content.

Accuracy and Rate Formula

Use the formula to measure a reader's accuracy and rate while reading aloud.

_____	−	_____	=	_____
words attempted in one minute		number of errors		words correct per minute (wcpm)

Name _____   Date _____

"Phyto-Power!"

Fill in the fact cards with details from "Phyto-Power!"

That's Amazing!

An amazing fact about _____

is _____

_____

I found it in the book _____

by _____

_____   _____
Name   Date

That's Amazing!

An amazing fact about _____

is _____

_____

I found it in the book _____

by _____

_____   _____
Name   Date

🗨 **Tell a partner which fact was your favorite and why.**

Name _____ Date _____

Respond and Extend

Compare Genres

Use the chart to compare "Phyto-Power!" with "Fish of the Future."

	Science article	Interview
Purpose Is the purpose to inform, entertain, persuade, or tell readers how to do something?		
Text structure	Main idea and details	Questions and answers
Text feature	**Photos** Yes **Tables** **Charts** **Illustrations** **Headings** **Maps** **Diagrams**	**Photos** Yes **Tables** **Charts** **Illustrations** **Headings** **Maps** **Diagrams**

Take turns with a partner. Ask each other questions about an interview or a science article.

© Cengage Learning, Inc.

3.19

Unit 3 | Nature's Webs

Grammar

The Make-It-Plural Game

Grammar Rules More Plurals Nouns

1. Some nouns are the same for "one" and "more than one."

   a grain of **sand** → *all the grains of* **sand**

2. Some nouns have special spellings for "more than one."

   one **mouse** → *two* **mice**

3. Collective nouns name groups of people or things.
   To make these nouns plural, add **-s** or **-es**.

   one **collection** *of seashells* → *two* **collections** *of seashells*

1. **Play with a partner.**
2. **Spin the spinner.**
3. **Change the noun to a plural noun. If the plural form is the same as the singular, say:** *same form.* **Say a sentence using the plural noun.**

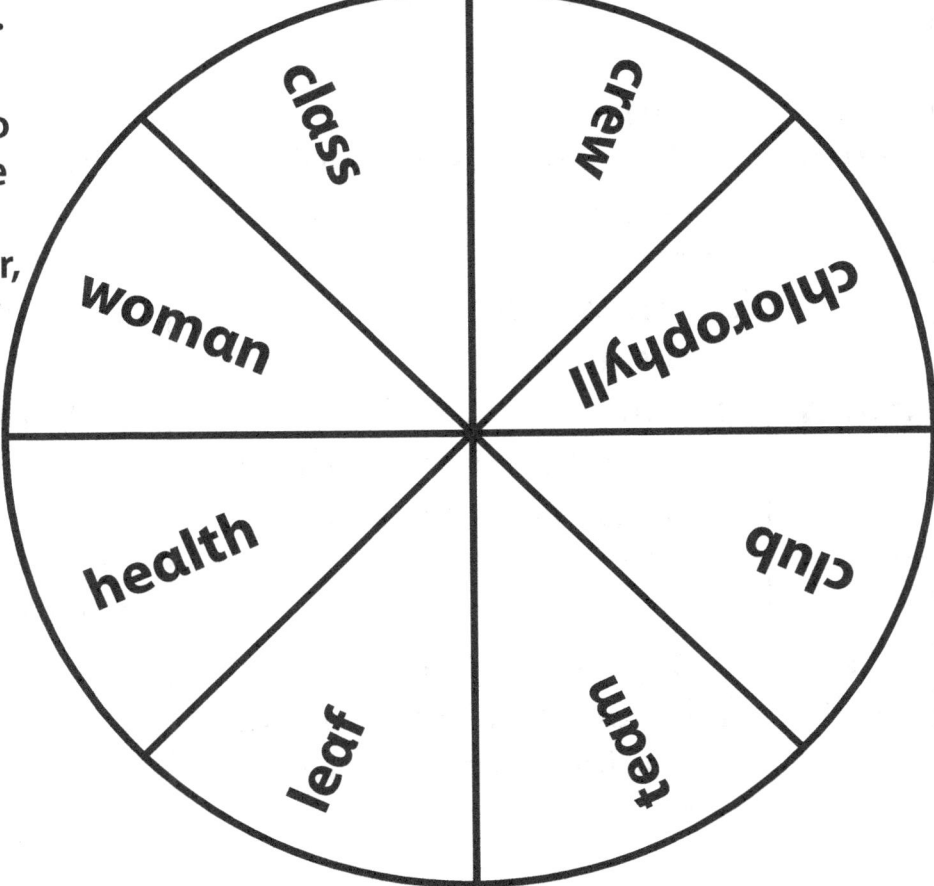

Make a Spinner

1. Place one loop of a paper clip over the center of the circle.
2. Push a sharp pencil through the loop and the paper.
3. Spin the paper clip around the pencil.

Organization

Writing is organized when it is easy to follow. All the ideas make sense together and flow from one idea to the next in an order that fits the writer's audience and purpose.

	Is the writing organized? Does it fit the audience and purpose?	Does the writing flow?
4 Wow!	❏ The writing is very well organized. ❏ It clearly fits both the writer's audience and purpose.	❏ The writing is smooth and logical. Each sentence flows into the next one.
3 Ahh.	❏ Most of the writing is organized. ❏ It mostly fits the writer's audience and purpose.	❏ Most of the writing is smooth. There are only a few sentences that do not flow logically.
2 Hmm.	❏ The writing is not well organized. ❏ It fits the writer's audience or the writer's purpose, but not both.	❏ Some of the writing is smooth. Many sentences do not flow smoothly.
1 Huh?	❏ The writing is not organized at all. ❏ It does not fit the writer's audience or purpose.	❏ The sentences do not flow smoothly or logically.

Name _____   Date _____

Chart

Complete a chart for your interview.

	Questions	Answers
Who?		
What?		
Where?		
When?		
Why?		
How?		

Writing Project

Revise

Use revision marks to make changes to this interview. Look for:

- a detailed introduction
- a logical organization

Revision Marks	
∧	Add
℘	Take out
⤾	Move to here
◯ SP	Check spelling
≡	Capitalize

Liz Fox

She has lots of experience with animals. She is a Wildlife Rescue volunteer. I asked her about opossums.

Q. Are opossums dangerous?

A. Opossums are shy creatures. However, they can carry rabies even when they do not look sick. So, if a person sees an opossum, it is best to leave it alone.

Q. What kind of animals are opossums?

A. Opossums are marsupials. they carry their young in pouches like kangaroos.

Q. What do opossums eat?

A. Opossums have a varied diet. They love to eat cat or dog food if it is available!

Name _____   Date _____

Edit and Proofread

Use revision marks to edit and proofread this interview. Look for:

- correct spelling of plural nouns
- correct spelling of irregular plural nouns
- correct capitalization and punctuation of proper and possessive nouns

Revision Marks	
∧	Add
℘	Take out
⬭⟋	Move to here
⬭ SP	Check spelling
≡	Capitalize
⸜∧	Add an apostrophe

Q. What does an opossum's look like?

A. Adult opossums are nearly two foot long (about 20 inchs) and can weigh up to ten pounds. An opossums long, hairless tail helps it hang from tree's. When frightened, it will often hiss and show its 50 sharp tooth.

Q. Ms. fox, what should a person do if he or she finds an injured opossum?

A. You could contact your local wildlife rescue organization. Volunteer's can often help injured opossum's and return them to the wild.

Unit Concept Map

Justice

**Make a concept map with the answers to the Big Question:
What is justice?**

What is justice?

Name _____ Date _____

TV Show Theme

Think about a hero in your favorite television show and fill in the theme chart.

TV show: _____

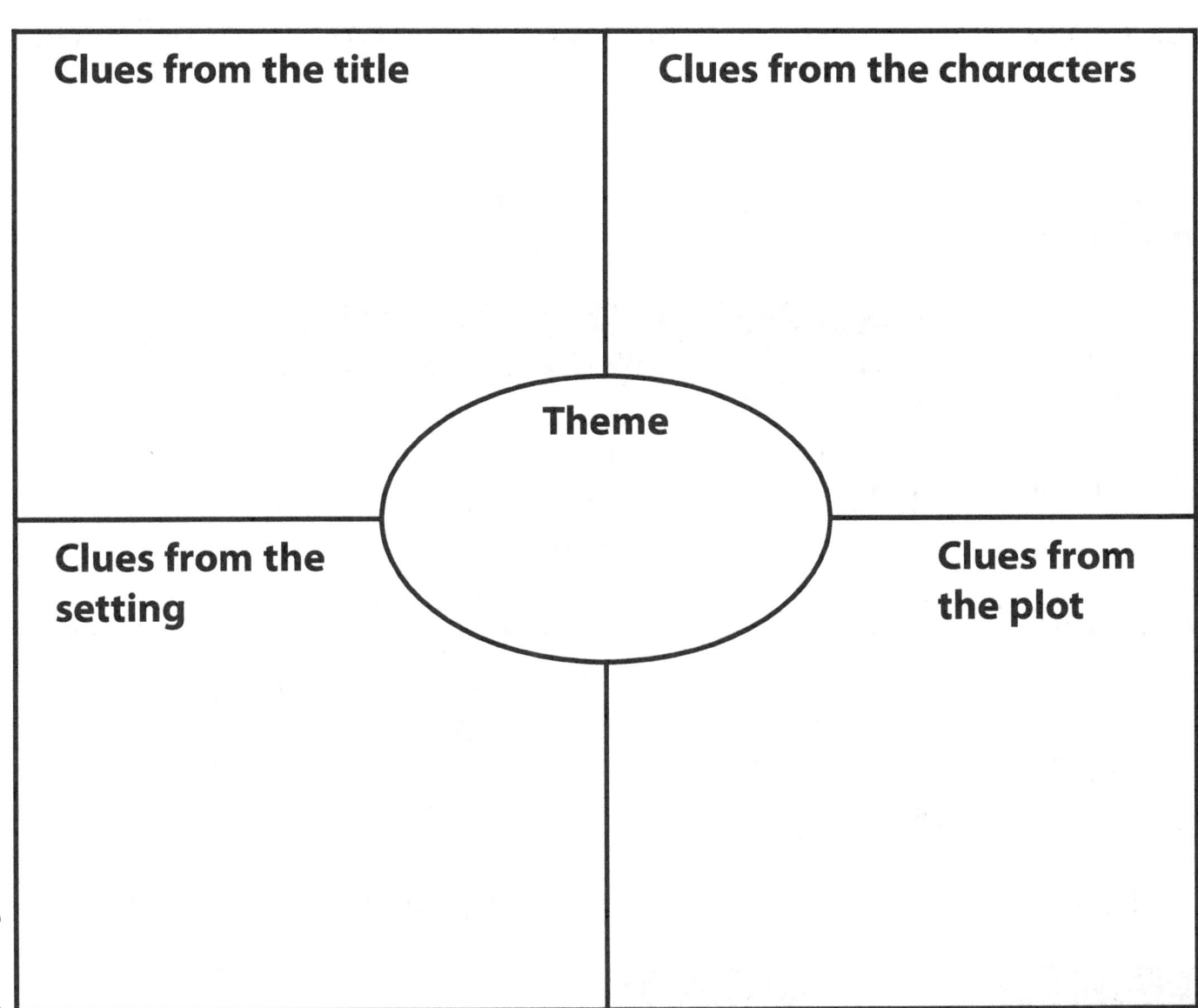

Clues from the title

Clues from the characters

Theme

Clues from the setting

Clues from the plot

Talk with a partner about a television show you have seen about a hero and decide what you think the theme is.

Grammar

The Action Game

Grammar Rules Present Tense Action Verbs

Present tense action verbs describe what people or things do *now*.

Examples: *A woman **speaks**. Manny and Maya **cheer**. The bell **rings**.*

Maria and Mark	We	miss	Ana and Lee	The woman	write
try		**How to play "The Action Game"**			lifts
Salvator		1. Play with a partner. Place two erasers on START.			The speaker
announce		2. Flip a coin. Move one space for heads. Move two spaces for tails. 3. Read the word. If it is a subject, use it in a sentence with a present			waits
Diego		tense verb. If it is a verb, use it in a sentence with a subject that agrees with it.			She
talk		4. Write your sentences on a sheet of paper. 5. The first one to reach FINISH wins.			They
START		FINISH	climb	He	reads

Key Points Reading

"Crossing Bok Chitto"

Listen as your teacher reads. Follow with your finger.

1

Bok Chitto was a river that separated the Choctaw from the plantations. One day, a Choctaw girl, Martha Tom, crossed the river. She walked on a secret stone path that lay just below the surface. Soon, she was lost. A boy named Little Mo led her home.

2

Little Mo's mother was to be sold. He wanted his family to cross Bok Chitto and escape, so he asked Martha Tom for help. The Choctaw women dressed in white and held candles. The guards pointed their guns, but they never fired. They thought they saw people walking on water.

3

Martha Tom led Little Mo's family across the river. People still remember that night. The Choctaw speak of Martha Tom's bravery. The dark-skinned people speak of Little Mo's faith. The white people speak of how seven enslaved people walked on water to freedom.

Grammar

Freedom

Grammar Rules Action Verbs: Present Progressive

1. A **present tense verb** tells about actions happening now.
2. **Present progressive verb phrases** talk about actions in progress.
3. Form the **present progressive** by adding the **present tense form** of the verb **be** to the **present participle**.
   Example: We **are walking**.

Replace each underlined verb with a present progressive verb phrase.

The enslaved people <u>work</u> _____ hard on the plantation.

They <u>dream</u> _____ of finding freedom. A Choctaw child

<u>plays</u> _____ nearby. She <u>thinks</u> _____ of helping

the enslaved people. As they walk in the forest, she <u>tells</u> _____

them about a plan.

The following week, someone on the plantation <u>helps</u> _____

the workers. The guards do not see what <u>happens</u> _____ .

The people <u>escape</u> _____ on a secret path. The plan is so

good that the people make it to freedom.

Name _____   Date _____

"Crossing Bok Chitto"

Reread "Crossing Bok Chitto" and fill in the theme chart.

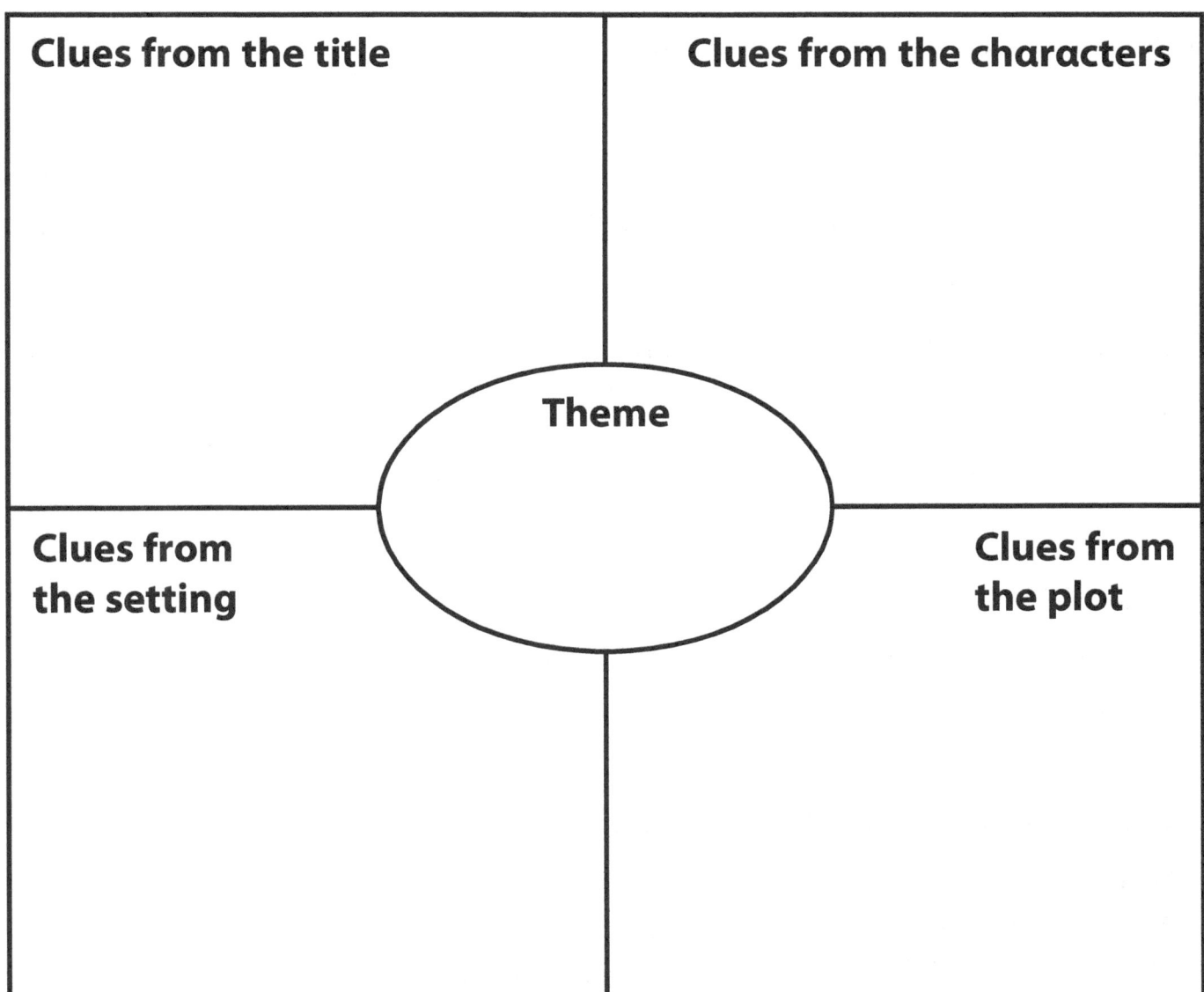

Clues from the title

Clues from the characters

Theme

Clues from the setting

Clues from the plot

Use your theme chart to retell the story to a partner.

Fluency

"Crossing Bok Chitto"

Use this passage to practice reading with proper expression.

Then one day, trouble came. Twenty enslaved people	8
were going to be sold. The men were called together to	19
listen to the names being read. Little Mo's mother was on	30
that list.	32
Little Mo's father wondered how to tell his family.	41
After supper, he motioned for them to be still. Feeling	51
his knees grow weak, he said, "Your mother has been	61
sold."	62
"Nooo!" she cried. The children began to cry, too.	71
"This is our last evening together!" he said. "Stop your	81
crying. I want every one of you to find something small	92
and precious to give your mother to remember you by."	102
No one moved.	105

From "Crossing Bok Chitto," page 239

Expression

B ☐ Does not read with feeling.

I ☐ Reads with some feeling, but does not match content.

A ☐ Reads with appropriate feeling for most content.

AH ☐ Reads with appropriate feeling for all content.

Accuracy and Rate Formula

Use the formula to measure a reader's accuracy and rate while reading aloud.

_____	–	_____	=	_____
words attempted in one minute		number of errors		words correct per minute (wcpm)

Name _____   Date _____

"Journey to Freedom"

List three interesting facts you read about in "Journey to Freedom."

That's a fact!

One interesting fact I read about is _____

_____

_____

Another interesting fact I read about is _____

_____

_____

One more interesting fact I read about is _____

_____

_____

Tell a partner which fact was the most interesting and why.

Name _____   Date _____

Compare Figurative Language

Read the figurative language used in "Crossing Bok Chitto" and "Journey to Freedom." Then write what the bold words help you picture.

"Journey to Freedom"	"Crossing Bok Chitto"
Enslaved people who were running away often traveled hundreds of miles to **reach** freedom. In my mind, I can see the people arriving at a safe place.	**Quick as a bird**, Little Mo flew across the stones. In my mind, I can see Little Mo hopping quickly across the stones.
As the runaways moved from **one station to the next, they were accompanied by a "conductor"** who made sure they arrived safely at the next destination. In my mind, I can see _____ _____ _____	Little Mo thought the music must be **the heartbeat of the earth itself.** In my mind, I can feel _____ _____ _____
	Martha Tom knew her mother **could cackle like a crow** when she was angry. In my mind, I can hear _____ _____ _____

Tell a partner what figurative language you liked in each selection. Talk about which selection was easier to "see" in your mind.

© Cengage Learning, Inc.

Grammar

Stories on the Wall

Grammar Rules Present Tense Action Verbs

1. Use a **present tense verb** if the action is happening now, or if it happens all the time.

2. Some action verbs show actions that you can't see.

3. In a sentence, the verb must agree with the subject of the sentence.

   Add **-s** to the verb when the subject is one person or thing.

   Do not add **-s** when the subject is more than one person or thing.

Complete each sentence with the correct form of the verb.

1. These people _____ (care, cares) about justice.

2. The town museum _____ (show, shows) this.

3. One whole room _____ (tell, tells) stories about justice.

4. We _____ (visit, visits) the museum every year.

5. My little brother _____ (read, reads) the stories on the wall.

Listen when a partner tells you a subject. Choose the right form of the present tense action verb for that subject. Together, make a sentence with the subject and verb.

Name _____   Date _____

Problems? Negotiate!

Use a sequence chain to write about something a partner negotiated.

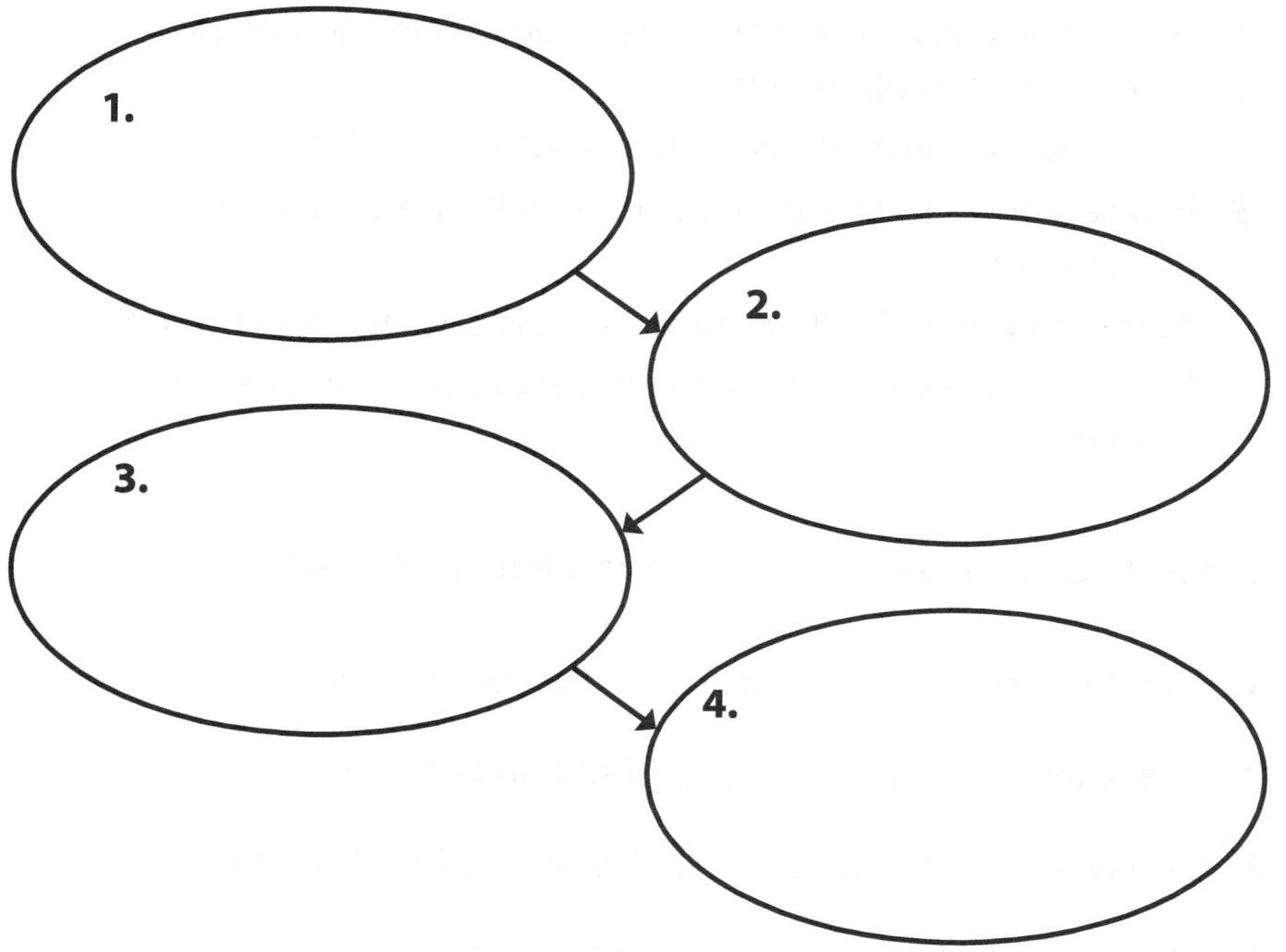

1.

2.

3.

4.

🟥 Tell a partner about something you negotiated. He or she writes the sequence of the negotiation in the sequence chain above.

© Cengage Learning, Inc.

Grammar

The Strike

Grammar Rules Verbs *am, is, are*

1. Use **am**, **is**, **are** to
- link the subject to a word in the predicate.
- tell about an action that is happening.
- come after the words **here** or **there**.
- make the contractions **I'm**, **you're**, **he's**, **she's**, **it's**, **we're**, **they're**.

2. The verb always agrees with the subject of the sentence.

Write am, is, are, I'm, you're, he's, we're, or they're to complete the passage.

Today _____ the day the workers _____ going on strike. I have never seen a strike, but _____ sure there are many good reasons for the strike. I _____ looking at the workers. All the workers _____ ready. One worker _____ speaking into a microphone. _____ telling the strikers to march for their rights.

They _____ marching in front of the store. There _____ many workers. _____ carrying signs. There _____ one worker marching near me. I ask him why they _____ on strike.

"We _____ asking for higher pay. _____ working in poor conditions," he says and then marches on.

▶ **Role-play the last four lines of the story with a partner. One partner asks why the workers are on strike. The other explains why. Switch roles and repeat.**

Name _____ Date _____

"The Troublemaker"

Listen as your teacher reads. Follow with your finger.

1

Nelson Mandela was born in Mvezo, South Africa. When he was very young, his family was forced to leave their village. Nelson never forgot the shock, pain, and injustice of the magistrate's decision.

2

While Nelson was at university, he joined a student council, which was trying to improve students' living conditions. The group organized a protest, and many students, including Nelson, were expelled.

3

In 1948, the South African government enacted the apartheid laws. These laws meant that South Africans who weren't white had fewer rights. For example, they were not allowed to vote, attend certain schools, or go outside after a certain hour.

4

Nelson and his friends used nonviolence to protest these laws. They were arrested several times, but they never gave up. They were sentenced to life in prison, but were released after 27 years. Nelson became the president of South Africa and worked hard to achieve peace.

Grammar

Complete It

Grammar Rules *have* and *has*

1. Use **has** when you tell about one other person or thing. **Has** becomes **'s** when you form a contraction.

2. Use **have** with all other subjects. **Have** becomes **'ve** when you form a contraction.

3. Use **has** and **have** as a helping verb with an **-ed** verb.

1. **Play with a partner.**
2. **Spin the spinner.**
3. **Complete the sentence with has or have.**

Make a Spinner

1. Place one loop of a paper clip over the center of the circle.
2. Push a sharp pencil through the loop and the paper.
3. Spin the paper clip around the pencil.

Name _____ Date _____

"The Troublemaker: The Story of Nelson Mandela"

Use the sequence chain to show what happened in "The Troublemaker: The Story of Nelson Mandela."

First, Nelson was born in the village of Mvezo.	Soon after, Nelson's father died, and Nelson went to live with his uncle.	Later,

Next, Nelson's family moved to Qunu.	Then,	Finally,

© Cengage Learning, Inc.

Use your sequence chain to retell the selection to a partner.

Fluency

"The Troublemaker: The Story of Nelson Mandela"

Use this passage to practice reading with proper phrasing.

Rolihlahla was born in the village of Mvezo, which lies in a	12
beautiful valley alongside the Mbhashe River. The village belonged	21
to the Thembu people. They kept animals, mostly cattle and sheep.	32
As a small boy, Rolihlahla helped his father care for the family's	44
animals. When he had finished for the day, he would play with the	57
other boys in the village. One of their favorite games was soccer. They	70
also practiced fighting with sticks, pretending to be great warriors from	81
generations past.	83
In the Xhosa language, Rolihlahla's name means "troublemaker."	91
Could this have been part of the reason why his fight for justice as a	106
grown-up got him into so much trouble?	113

From "The Troublemaker: The Story of Nelson Mandela," page 265

Phrasing

B ☐ Rarely pauses while reading the text.

I ☐ Occasionally pauses while reading the text.

A ☐ Frequently pauses at appropriate points in the text.

AH ☐ Consistently pauses at all appropriate points in the text.

Accuracy and Rate Formula

Use the formula to measure accuracy and rate while reading aloud.

_____	–	_____	=	_____
words attempted in one minute		number of errors		words correct per minute (wcpm)

Name _____ Date _____

Reading Options

"Sisters Fighting for the Oceans"

Complete this reflection journal as you read the social studies article.

Page	My question	The answer

Talk with a partner about how environmental justice can help people.

Name _____   Date _____

Compare Literary Language

Compare the different writing features used in "The Troublemaker" and "Sisters Fighting for the Oceans."

	"The Troublemaker"	"Sisters Fighting for the Oceans"
Facts and information	p. 275	p. 282 The island produces enough plastic every day to fill a 14-story building.
Foreshadowing	p. 265 Rolihlahla's name means "troublemaker." Could this have been the reason why his fight for justice got him into so much trouble?	p. 283
Imagery	p. 265	p. 282

Take turns with a partner. Describe a place you know using imagery.

Grammar

Bus Strike

Grammar Rules Forms of *be* and *have*

1. For yourself, use **am** or **have**.

2. When you tell about another person or a thing, use **is** or **has**.

3. For yourself and one or more people, use **are** or **have**.

4. When you tell about other people and things, use **are** or **have**.

5. For linking verbs, use **am**, **is**, and **are** to link the subject to a word in the predicate.

6. For helping verbs, use **am**, **is**, and **are** with **-ing** verbs and **has** or **have** with **-ed** verbs.

Write the correct forms of be and have. If a subject is also needed in the sentence, use a contraction.

A news reporter _____ just arrived at the bus headquarters. Drivers _____ unhappy, and they _____ decided to strike. The reporter interviewed the spokesperson for the drivers. She asked, "Why _____ you protesting?"

The spokesperson replied, "We _____ all doing the same job, but some drivers earn more than others. We _____ asked for equal pay, but the officials _____ not agreed. So, _____ decided to strike until our demand for equal pay _____ met."

▬▬▶ **Pick a form of be and a form of have and write two new sentences. Use a contraction in one of the sentences. Read your sentences to a partner.**

© Cengage Learning, Inc.

Name _____ Date _____

Organization

Writing is organized when it is easy to follow. All the ideas make sense together and flow from one idea to the next in an order that fits the writer's audience and purpose.

	Is the writing organized? Does it fit the audience and purpose?	Does the writing flow?
4 Wow!	❑ The writing is very well organized. ❑ It clearly fits both the writer's audience and purpose.	❑ The writing is smooth and logical. Each sentence flows into the next one.
3 Ahh.	❑ Most of the writing is organized. ❑ It mostly fits the writer's audience and purpose.	❑ Most of the writing is smooth. There are only a few sentences that do not flow logically.
2 Hmm.	❑ The writing is not well organized. ❑ It fits the writer's audience or the writer's purpose, but not both.	❑ Some of the writing is smooth. Many sentences do not flow smoothly.
1 Huh?	❑ The writing is not organized at all. ❑ It does not fit the writer's audience or purpose.	❑ The sentences do not flow smoothly or logically.

Writing Project

Brainstorm Your Topic

Use the chart to brainstorm possible topics for your research report and circle the topic that is most interesting to you.

Event	When did it happen?	Who was involved?

Writing Project

Source Cards

Create a source card for each source.

Title:	Card number:
Author:	
Publication information:	
Library call number or website address:	

Title:	Card number:
Author:	
Publication information:	
Library call number or website address:	

Writing Project

Outline

Use your note cards to create an outline. Use Arabic numbers (1, 2, 3) to add more details under your supporting points.

I.

    A.

    B.

    C.

II.

    A.

    B.

    C.

III.

    A.

    B.

    C.

Name ______________________________ Date ________________

Writing Project

Revise

Use revision marks to make changes to these paragraphs. Look for:

- **an order that makes sense**
- **the writer's own words**

Revision Marks	
^	Add
	Take out
	Move to here

Dr. Héctor P. García

Dr. Héctor Pérez García fought for his rights. Dr. García was a doctor. He was also a hero in World War II. He founded a group called American GI Forum. He believed that everyone should have the same rights.

There was a time when Dr. García's wife and daughter were not welcomed in a café. In south Texas, Mexican-Americans were treated unfairly. Dr. García said, "We had segregated schools, segregated campuses, segregated hospitals."

Dr. García's name would be forever interspersed with the names of heroes in the annals of history.

Name _____ Date _____

Edit and Proofread

Use revision marks to edit and proofread these paragraphs and source list. Look for:

- subject-verb agreement
- words with suffixes spelled correctly
- correct punctuation and capitalization in a source list

Revision Marks	
∧	Add
℘	Take out
⬭⟋	Move to here
≡	Capital letter

After Felix Longoria was killed in World War II, the funeral director in his hometown did not allow his body to be in the funeral home. Longoria's wife talked to Dr. Garcia. With his help, Felix Longoria became the first Mexican-American to receive a hero's buryal in Arlington National Cemetery.

Dr. Garcia's organization continue to help many Mexican-Americans get justice. Garcia are a true hero.

Sources

Allsup, V. Carl. "Felix longoria Affair." *The New handbook of Texas.* 1996. Print.

Felts, Jeff. "justice for My people: The dr. Héctor p García Story." Corpus Christi: KEDT-Public Television. 2009. <http://www.justiceformypeople.org/index.html>

Garcia, Ignacio M. *"Héctor P. garcía: In Relentless Pursuit of Justice."* houston: Arte Público Press, 2002.

Photographic Credits

1.1 (r) Photosindia Collection/Getty Images. 1.14 (t) Bill Bachmann/Alamy Stock Photo. (c) Keith Brofsky/ Getty Images. (b) Colin McPherson/Getty Images. 2.13 (t) Thomas Culhane/National Geographic Image Collection. (cl) Tatiana Popova/Shutterstock.com. (tc) acilo/Getty Images. (bc) Thomas Culhane/National Geographic Image Collection. 3.1 (t) Stephen Frink/DigitalVision/Getty Images. (tc) Arco Peter/Getty Images. (c) Jupiterimages/Getty Images. (bc) Roland Birke/Photolibrary/Getty Images. (b) Scenics & Science/Alamy Stock Photo. 3.14 (t) Courtesy of Tierney Thys. (c) Mike Johnson Marine Natural History Photography. 4.13 (t) Hein Von Horstein/Getty Images. (tc) Terence Spencer/Getty Images. (bc) Africa Media Online/akg-images. (b) Trinity Mirror/Mirrorpix/Alamy Stock Photo.

Division

Multipli

$$6 \times 5 = 30$$
$$6 \times 6 = 36$$
$$6 \times 7 = 42$$
$$6 \times 8 = 48$$
$$6 \times 9 = 54$$
$$6 \times 10 = 60$$